THE 101st AIRBORNE IN NORMANDY

JUNE 1944

CASEMATE | ILLUSTRATED

CASEMATE | ILLUSTRATED

THE 101ST AIRBORNE IN NORMANDY

JUNE 1944

YVES BUFFETAUT

with Yoann Marlière

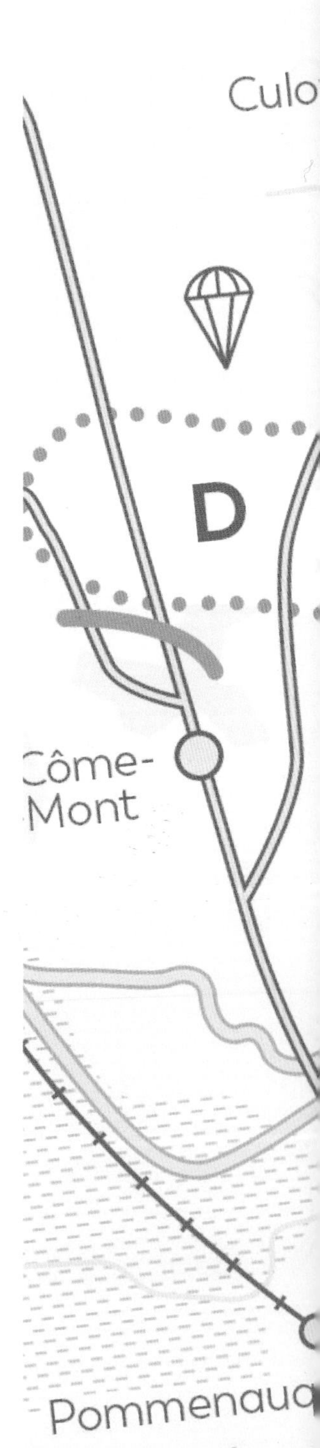

Print Edition: ISBN 978-1-61200-5232
Digital Edition: ISBN 978-1-61200-5249

This book is published in cooperation with and under license from Sophia Histoire & Collections. Originally published in French as Militaria Hors-Serie No 95, © Histoire & Collections 2015

Typeset, design and additional material © Casemate Publishers 2018
Translation by Hannah McAdams
Design by Paul Hewitt, Battlefield Design
Color artwork by Eric Schwartz © Histoire & Collections
Photo retouching and separations by Remy Spezzano
Additional text by Steven Smith
Printed and bound by Megaprint, Turkey

CASEMATE PUBLISHERS (US)
Telephone (610) 853-9131
Fax (610) 853-9146
Email: casemate@casematepublishers.com
www.casematepublishers.com

CASEMATE PUBLISHERS (UK)
Telephone (01865) 241249
Fax (01865) 794449
Email: casemate-uk@casematepublishers.co.uk
www.casematepublishers.co.uk

Vierville
Angoville
-au-Plain
Cesarbourg
Carentan
le Mesnil

Contents

Timeline of Events: June 1944

The 101st Airborne Division served as a spearhead of the Allied invasion from the dark early hours of D-Day to the fall of Carentan on June 13. Afterward it was transferred to VIII Corps and took up defensive positions on the Cotentin peninsula until it was relieved from frontline duty at the end of the month and shipped back to England to rest and refit.

1 2 3 4 5 6 7 8 9 10 11 12 13 14 15

JUNE 5: After a 24-hour delay due to poor weather, the first waves of the 101st take off at around 23:00.

JUNE 6–D-DAY: The 101st Airborne are dropped into occupied France. The liberation of Europe begins.

JUNE 10: After fierce fighting for a few days against German defenses along the Douve, the 101st advances across the causeway toward Carentan, led by the 502 PIR.

JUNE 12: Following a three-pronged assault by the 101st, the German defenders withdraw from Carentan, leaving a rearguard to delay the Airborne's pursuit. The 101st mops up the town and emerges on the other side to face a new onslaught.

JUNE 13: The 17th SS PzG Division launches a counterattack from the southwest to retake Carentan. The 101st barely holds on in the face of enemy panzergrenadiers and SPGs, until elements of the 2nd Armored Division arrive from the beaches to even the odds and restore the line.

JUNE 15: The 101st is transferred to the newly arrived U.S. VIII Corps, and placed in defensive positions guarding the left flank of Joe Collins' advancing VII Corps.

JUNE 27: The 101st are withdrawn from the front lines and replaced by elements of the 83rd and 90th Infantry Divisions. After briefly occupying positions around Cherbourg, they return to England to await their next mission.

16 17 18 19 20 21 22 23 24 25 26 27 28 29 30

Background and Formation of the 101st Airborne Division

"The 101st Airborne Division . . . has no history, but it has a rendezvous with destiny."

—Major General William C. Lee, August 19, 1942

Just days before the Armistice concluded the Great War in November 1918, the 101st Division was put on the U.S. Army's drawing board; however, with the end of hostilities the division never fully came into being. It was not until America's entrance into World War II that the unit became activated: this time as one of the Army's first airborne divisions.

The paratroopers of the 101st would all be volunteers, and word was spread that only the bravest, most daring, and physically fit young men need apply. They would become among the most highly trained combat troops in the world, with the promise to be at the cutting edge of the Allies' war against the Axis.

In this scene captured before June 5, paratroopers of the 101st Airborne are being briefed and trained. Their equipment is lying on the ground. (NARA)

As the 101st Airborne Division's first commander, Maj. Gen. William ("Bill") Lee announced to the troops upon their formation in August 1942:

> "Due to the nature of our armament, and the tactics in which we shall perfect ourselves, we shall be called upon to carry out operations of far-reaching military importance and we shall habitually go into action when the need is immediate and extreme. Let me call your attention to the fact that our badge is the great American eagle. This is a fitting emblem for a division that will crush its enemies by falling upon them like a thunderbolt from the skies."

General William C. Lee

Born in 1895, William C. ("Bill") Lee graduated from North Carolina State College (ROTC) and was commissioned a lieutenant in 1917, in time to lead an AEF platoon, and then a company, in France during the Great War. Remaining in the peacetime Army, he was impressed during a tour of Europe by the Germans' development of an airborne force, and advocated that the United States do the same.

At first his enthusiasm fell on deaf ears—his immediate superior told him, "No American soldier is ever going to have little enough sense to jump out of an airplane . . ."—until FDR himself caught wind of the Germans' airborne concept and asked the Army what they were doing about it.

Lee then became commander of the U.S. Army's first jump school, at Fort Benning, and in August 1942 was named commander of the new 101st Airborne Division. When the division shipped to England, Lee participated in the planning for D-Day and intended to jump with his men as the spearhead of the invasion. In February 1944, however, he suffered a drastic illness and had to relinquish his command to Maxwell Taylor.

Nevertheless, as the "father" of the U.S. airborne, Lee was remembered fondly by his paratroopers, many of whom shouted "Bill Lee" (instead of "Geronimo") when they jumped into the black skies over Normandy. Back in the States, Lee was still able to follow the exploits of his 101st as they wrote an unsurpassed record of heroism in the war.

Never fully recovering from his illness, Lee passed away in 1949, at age 53. His important legacy, however, endures today, in part through the General William C. Lee Airborne Museum in his hometown of Dunn, North Carolina.

Shortly before the landings, Waco and Horsa gliders and C-47 transport planes were packed in tightly at this English base. It took more than 400 aircraft to carry 6,000 paratroopers. (NARA)

E Company, 506th Parachute Infantry Regiment, at Fort Brass, North Carolina, in September 1943. Easy Company would be made famous by Stephen Ambrose's book *Band of Brothers* and the TV mini-series of the same name. (Rights reserved)

Planning and Preparation

As the invasion of Normandy approached in the spring of 1944, the potential of airborne warfare was still a matter of debate within the Allied high command. The previous record of airborne operations had ranged from bloody success to utter fiasco, with a few gallant reinforcement missions thrown in. The Germans, who had pioneered airborne attacks, had given up on the concept after suffering horrendous casualties in their invasion of Crete. The American airborne had suffered hundreds of casualties to friendly fire in Sicily, along with badly scattered drops. Missions in Italy had gone better, but without attempts at deep penetration. By the time of the Normandy invasion the Allies had assembled the men and machines to launch the war's largest airborne operation yet; however, this time the objective was also the most dangerous: breaking through Hitler's Atlantic Wall in France.

While nearly everyone agreed that the airborne divisions would be essential for the success of the Normandy invasion, during the planning stages the American military was torn between two doctrines of thought: that of General George C. Marshall, Chief of Staff in Washington, and that of General Dwight D. Eisenhower, Commander of the Supreme Headquarters Allied Expeditionary Force (SHAEF). In February 1944, it was decided that the airborne forces would indeed play an important part, but one of a purely tactical nature, rather than the strategic role that Marshall had envisaged them undertaking.

Marshall's stance was not a new one. In August 1943, he had already proposed it to the British general Sir Frederick Morgan, who, at the time, was chief of staff of COSSAC (Chief of Staff to Supreme Allied Commander), the predecessor of SHAEF. Marshall's doctrine was based upon one simple question: "Why not reverse everything and have the parachutists and airborne troops as the principal force,

The "Band of Brothers"

Although the men of Easy Co., 506th PIR would be the first to affirm they were neither better nor worse than other paratroopers in the 101st Airborne, their wartime saga—as illuminated in literature and TV—does serve as a microcosm of the Screaming Eagles' experience in World War II. After Normandy they went on to fight in Market Garden and the Battle of the Bulge, and ended the war occupying Hitler's Eagle's Nest.

On the eve of D-Day a Stars and Stripes photographer found these paratroopers donning the hairstyles and warpaint of Na American warriors. They were members of a demolition squad attached to HQ Co., 1st Battalion, 506th PIR. Notorious for ra rousing, this squad was led by an Oklahoman named Jake McNiece (at right, above) and were known within the 101st as the Thirteen. The squad was said to be the inspiration for the 1960s Hollywood blockbuster, "The Dirty Dozen." (Rights reserved)

Waco and Horsa gliders, and C-47 transport planes packed in this English base. (NARA)

In Profile: General Dwight D. Eisenhower

It is an irony that the commander of Supreme Headquarters Allied Expeditionary Force (SHAEF) was a man who had never previously led troops in combat. Yet under Dwight D. Eisenhower, SHAEF achieved a record of nearly unbroken success, and after the war it was dissolved, having only had him as its commander.

Eisenhower was born in 1890 and raised in Kansas. He graduated from West Point in 1915, and like other young officers yearned for a combat role when America entered the Great War two years later. But his training and organizational skills kept him confined to the States, and the end of the war found him at Camp Colt on the old Gettysburg battlefield, where he was charged with organizing America's first tank corps. Afterward he excelled in staff positions alongside MacArthur, Marshall and other future luminaries, and acquired a special mentor in General Fox Conner, Pershing's former chief of staff.

In World War II the selfless Eisenhower was a compromise choice to serve as commander of the joint Anglo-American force in the Mediterranean, and in a theater rife with rivalries, he issued a dictum to U.S. commanders not to speak ill of their British counterparts. Named head of SHAEF in December 1943, Eisenhower became intimately involved in the planning for D-Day, and was willing to accept entire responsibility had it failed. After the Allied lodgment on the Continent he switched his HQ to France and assumed direct command of all Allied forces.

After the war his diplomatic and political skills were proven anew when he became president of the United States, 1953–1960, under the campaign slogan, "I like Ike."

Generals Eisenhower and Marshall with Mrs Eisenhower. (NARA)

Ike and Marshall

Though George Marshall would have preferred the direct command role of Eisenhower, ten years his junior, the two of them comprised a formidable team during WWII. This was first demonstrated after the formation of the Combined Chiefs of Staff, when Marshall was able to hold his own with the more experienced, war-tested British. Eisenhower meantime balanced the views of British field commanders. Though compromising with the British on issues such as the Mediterranean, the Americans stuck to their guns for a cross-Channel invasion at the earliest possible date, resulting in the invasion of Normandy.

with the naval effort as support?" Morgan, not wishing to take sides, hedged his bets and referred the proposal to Air Marshal Trafford Leigh-Mallory, who would be commanding the airborne operations during the landings. Leigh-Mallory was not at all convinced by Marshall's arguments, and set the issue aside.

The Airborne Controversy

In February 1944, Marshall tried again, and sent General Frederick W. Evans, commander of First Troop Carrier Command, and Colonel Bruce W. Bidwell, of the Operations Division of the War Department, to London. They took with them a letter, in Marshall's own hand, dated February 10, to be delivered to Eisenhower. Marshall's note was written in a direct and unceremonious manner, which almost certainly exasperated Eisenhower:

> My dear Eisenhower:
>
> Up to the present time I have not felt that we have properly exploited air power as regards its combination with ground troops. We have lacked planes, of course, in which to transport men and supplies, but our most serious deficiency I think has been a lack in conception. Our procedure has been a piecemeal proposition with each commander grabbing at a piece to assist his particular phase of the operation, very much as they did with tanks and as they tried to do with the airplane itself. It is my opinion that we now possess the means to give a proper application to this phase of air power in a combined operation.
>
> I might say that it was my determination in the event I went to England to do this, even to the extent that should the British be in opposition I would carry it out exclusively with American troops. I am not mentioning this as pressure on you but merely to give you some idea of my own conclusions in the matter.
>
> With the foregoing in mind and seeing the proposed plan for OVERLORD in Airborne troops, General Arnold had Brigadier General Fred Evans, Commanding General of the Troop Carrier Command, and Colonel Bruce Bidwell, the OPD Airborne Consultant, make a study of the proposition for OVERLORD.
>
> They first presented to us Plan A, which utilizes the airborne troops in three major groups with mission to block the movement of hostile reserve divisions as now located. This was not acceptable to me. On paper it was fine; but on the

A chaplain of the 439th Troop Carrier Group watches as a C-47 returns from a mission on June 7, 1944. (NARA)

General Marshall (center) with General "Hap" Arnold, commander of the US Army Air Force. (NARA)

ground it would be too few men at the critical points with almost the certainty that the Germans would circumvent them in vicious fighting. I saw exactly this happen in the great German offensive of March, 1918. In preparation for the attack the Allies organized their forces in depth, the various points of resistance being staggered. On a map it was perfect pin-ball set-up to disrupt the enemy's effort. On the ground it was a series of quick collapses where small groups of lonely men were cut off and surrendered.

I then had them reconsider their plan more in accordance with my conception of the application of airborne troops on a large scale. This resulted in two plans.

Plan B—This establishes an air-head in the general Argentan area approximately thirty miles inland from Caen, with mission to seize two airfields and restrict the movement of hostile reserves that threaten the beach landing area from the east and southeast.

This plan is not satisfactory to me because the airfields are small and not capable of rapid expansion and we could not take heavy planes in to provide a quick build-up. Moreover, holding this particular locality would not pose a major strategic threat to the Germans.

Plan C—Establishes an air-head in keeping with my ideas on the subject, one that can be quickly established and developed to great strength in forty-eight hours. The area generally south of Evreux has been selected because of four excellent airfields.

In Profile:
General George C. Marshall

Born in 1880 to a family of old Virginia lineage, George Marshall graduated from VMI in 1901, and soon was commanding a company during the Philippines insurrection. Upon America's entry into the Great War he was assigned to AEF HQ in France, and as an aide to General Pershing helped plan America's first great foreign campaign, the Meuse-Argonne Offensive.

Between the wars Marshall served in various staff and command roles, rising steadily through the ranks until in 1939 he was named the U.S. Army's Chief of Staff. When war broke out in both Europe and the Far East, America began a crash program to enlarge, train, and modernize its military. After Pearl Harbor brought America in with both feet, Roosevelt felt he could not spare Marshall from Washington. Marshall continued to exert a firm-handed influence on strategy, however, especially through his younger subordinate Eisenhower, as they planned the daring invasion to crack Hitler's Atlantic Wall in France.

After the war Marshall became Truman's Secretary of State, and lent his name to the aid plan that helped to resurrect Europe. He switched to the role of Secretary of Defense at the start of the Korean War when another fast remobilization became necessary. Marshall passed away in 1959 at his home in Virginia.

Paratroopers of the 2nd Battalion, 502nd PIR, pose in front of their C-47 at Greenham Common. (Rights reserved)

> This plan appeals to me because I feel that it is a true vertical envelopment and would create such a strategic threat to the Germans that it would call for a major revision of their defensive plans. It should be a complete surprise, an invaluable asset of any such plan. It would directly threaten the crossings of the Seine as well as the city of Paris. It should serve as a rallying point for considerable elements of the French underground.
>
> In effect, we would be opening another front in France and your buildup would be tremendously increased in rapidity.
>
> The trouble with this plan is that we have never done anything like this before, and frankly, that reaction makes me tired. Therefore I should like you to give these young men an opportunity to present the matter to you personally before your Staff tears it to ribbons. Please believe that, as usual, I do not want to embarrass you with undue pressure. I merely wish to be certain that you have viewed this possibility on a definite planning basis.
>
> Faithfully yours,
>
> G. C. Marshall

This letter did not convince Eisenhower, who responded with an even longer missive in which he addressed Marshall's points one by one. The crux of his view, tactfully submitted, read:

Several C-47s in England on June 7, 1944. The aircraft were painted with black-and-white stripes to facilitate their identification. These belonged to the 439th Troop Carrier Group, and behind them are a number of CG-4 Wacos. (NARA)

Mechanics use a crane to attach a Waco's wing at a British base. (NARA)

German Defenses

In the ETO, every experience gained by the Allied airborne also meant a lesson learned by the Germans in how to oppose them. The Germans knew well that concentrated night-time drops were difficult, yet daytime drops into the teeth of AA fire in built-up zones like Normandy were unlikely. Their preparation prior to D-Day was to spread their defenses, flooding likely drop zones and planting stakes, often topped with mines, in areas suitable for gliders. Machine-gun nests and quick-reaction patrols were also sprinkled throughout the area.

The build-up of Omaha Beach on 8 June 1944. This is what the advance landings of the airborne divisions were designed to protect. (NARA)

A man of IX Troop Carrier Command attaches a glider's traction cable to a C-47. (NARA)

In Profile: Materiel Used by the 101st Airborne

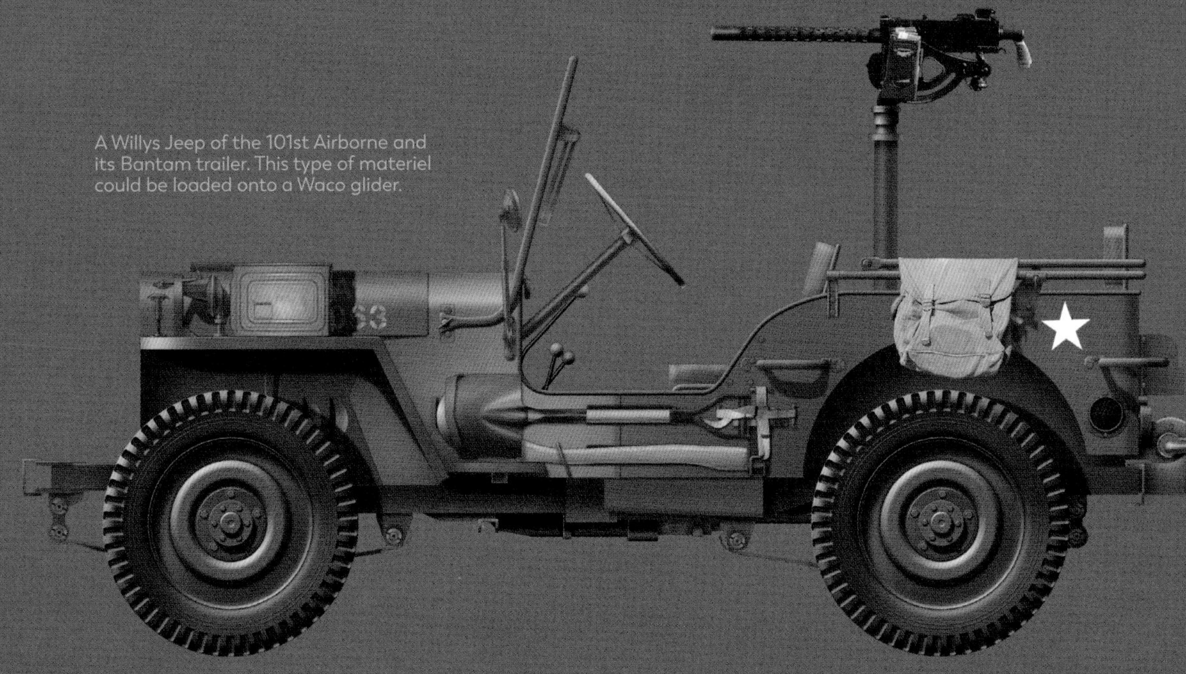

A Willys Jeep of the 101st Airborne and its Bantam trailer. This type of materiel could be loaded onto a Waco glider.

Airborne troops fought primarily as light infantry, but they did possess heavier equipment to be transported by gliders following the initial wave of paratroopers. Before dawn on D-Day, Operation Chicago called for 52 gliders to bring in 25 Jeeps, 16 antitank guns, a small bulldozer, and nearly 15 tons of ordnance, communications, and medical equipment.

Due to crashes and landing zones covered by enemy fire, the mission was not a complete success, as the paras were initially only able to retrieve three Jeeps and six guns, plus various containers. In the meantime, men of the 101st commandeered French farm carts and captured German vehicles for mobility. A follow-up glider mission, Operation *Keokuk*, after dusk on D-Day, brought in more much-needed equipment.

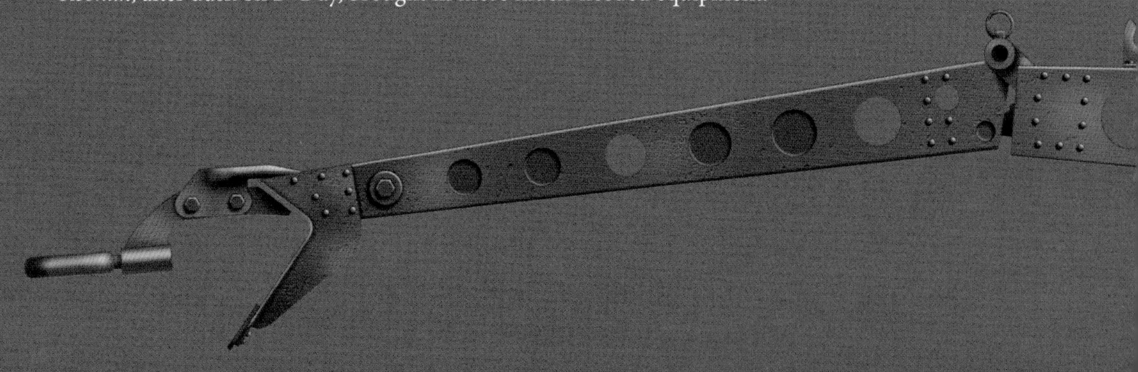

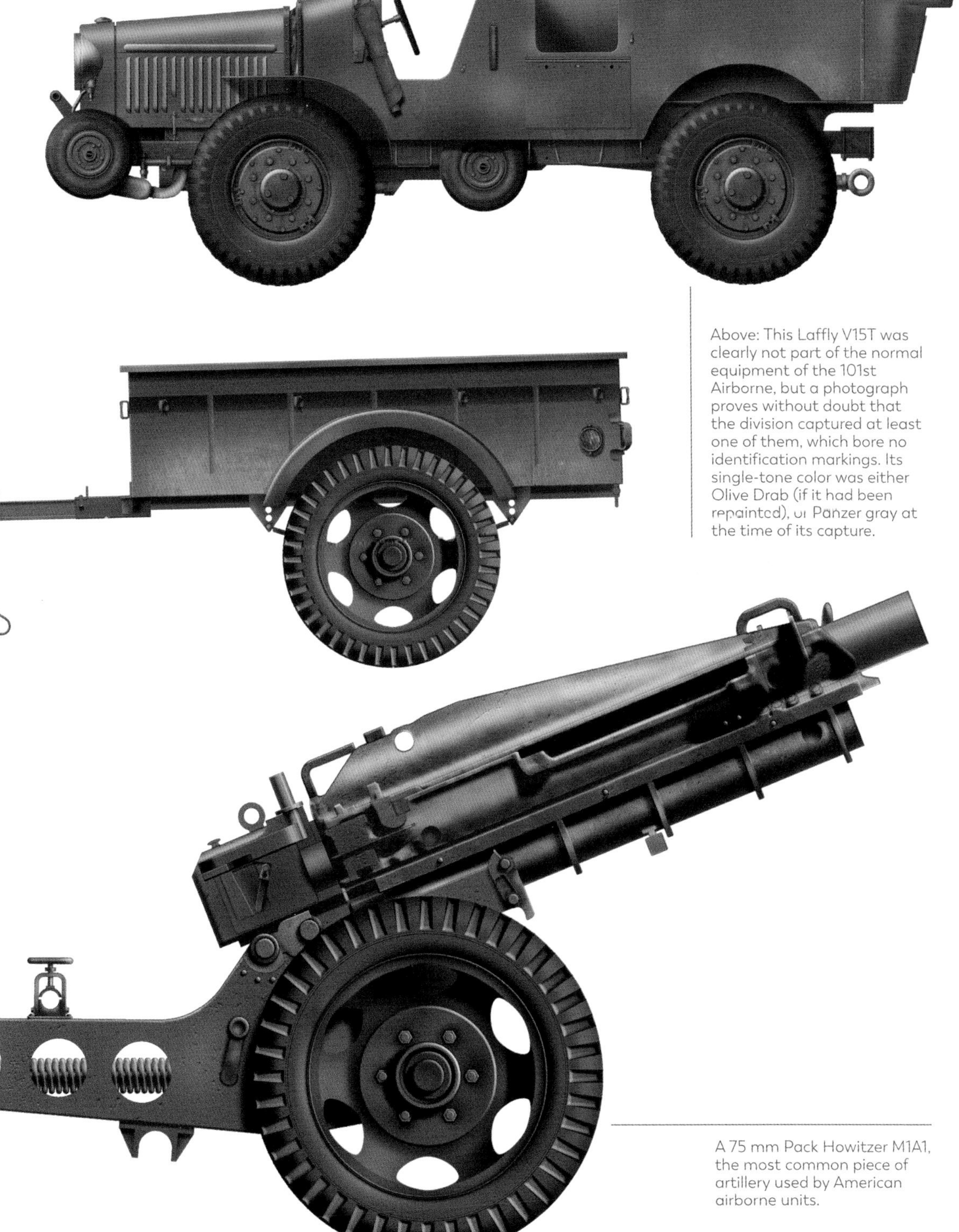

Above: This Laffly V15T was clearly not part of the normal equipment of the 101st Airborne, but a photograph proves without doubt that the division captured at least one of them, which bore no identification markings. Its single-tone color was either Olive Drab (if it had been repainted), or Panzer gray at the time of its capture.

A 75 mm Pack Howitzer M1A1, the most common piece of artillery used by American airborne units.

A Waco glider in flight, towed by a C-47 (out of shot). This type of aircraft could carry 13 soldiers, or a Jeep, or a 75mm howitzer. (NARA)

> **My initial reaction to the specific proposal is that I agree thoroughly with the conception but disagree with the timing. Mass in vertical envelopments is sound—but since this kind of an enveloping force is immobile on the ground, the collaborating force must be strategically and tactically mobile. So the time for the mass vertical envelopment is after the beach-head has been gained and a striking force built up!**

Eisenhower then developed his arguments, noting especially that the Allies would quickly encounter a decisive tactical crisis after the landings: the difficulty of establishing a strong bridgehead of at least one good port, which would allow reinforcements to arrive continuously on the continent. To establish this bridgehead and face this first crisis, Eisenhower would need all his forces, including the airborne divisions.

He then gave the example of Italy, where there were fewer roads than in France, and where the Germans were nonetheless able to send in large numbers of reserves despite the aerial superiority of the Allies. In France, the problem would be even worse, and even an airborne mass would be in great difficulty if it were isolated and could be attacked separately.

He noted that the Germans did not seem to take seriously the risk of a strategic encirclement and cited the landings at Anzio, Italy, which should have prompted the Germans to retreat toward the north, but served no purpose in the end because the troops that landed were too static, as the airborne divisions would be if they were sent to the Evreux sector. In Eisenhower's opinion, the bridgehead at Anzio had only survived due to the total naval

A freight cargo is loaded onto a C-47 at an American base. The whole front of the fuselage is unpainted aluminum, while its tail (and perhaps its wings) are painted in Olive Drab. Just visible in the background is a B-17 Flying Fortress. (NARA)

supremacy of the Allies. He was convinced that an isolated airborne bridgehead would quickly be destroyed, and his priority for Normandy was ensuring that there was sufficient force to address the resistance he knew the amphibious assault would face on the beaches. In short, while the airborne troops would abet the seaborne landings, the fully equipped troops coming ashore would be needed to soon support the airborne.

The matter was settled: Eisenhower would neither adopt nor take into account Marshall's idea, particularly because of the danger posed by the proximity of the German air bases in the Paris area.

A long column of C-47s preparing for takeoff. The Luftwaffe was no longer able to reach British air bases, which is why so many aircraft are out on the airfield. (NARA)

Soldiers of the 101st Airborne Division unload equipment from a Horsa glider during a training maneuver in January 1944. (NARA)

The 101st Airborne in England

The 101st Airborne Division, commanded by General William C. ("Bill") Lee, arrived in England in late summer 1943 to train for the landings planned for the following spring. On paper, the 101st comprised the 327th Glider Infantry Regiment; 401st Glider Infantry Regiment; and 502nd Parachute Infantry Regiment (PIR). In June 1943, the division was reinforced with another parachute regiment, the 506th, and then the 501st Parachute Infantry Regiment in January 1944. The 82nd Airborne Division only arrived in Northern Ireland in December 1943, having previously been deployed in the Mediterranean.

In February 1944, Bill Lee, known as the "father" of the US Airborne, suffered a heart attack and was forced to relinquish command of the 101st. He was replaced by Brigadier General Maxwell D. Taylor, who had formerly commanded the 82nd Airborne's artillery.

The airborne officers considered training for combat to be more important than jump training. So, in order to limit the number of "real" jumps, which took a long time to set up and were costly to implement, troopers undertook "fake" jumps: launching themselves off moving trucks, where the impact on landing was judged to be close enough to the real thing for training purposes. Jump schools were created in May 1944, complete with dedicated "jump towers," and sufficient aircraft were made available to undertake large-scale maneuvers, but the unit commanders preferred to push ground-based fighting, judging that men would be injured during jumps from actual aircraft.

Pathfinders

The most dangerous job in the airborne naturally fell to the most elite men, and in addition, the best pilots of Troop Carrier Command were assigned to the role. Together their job was to precede the invasion behind enemy lines to mark out the drop zones for the planes and paratroopers that followed. In Normandy, however, theory collided with practice, due to faulty drops or Germans already on or around the DZs. In the end only two of the six parachute regiments landed with proper organization, the rest seriously scattered across the countryside.

The Airborne Transport Force

Numerous transport divisions were needed for the transportation of the two airborne divisions. With an original cadre of six officers from I Troop Carrier Command (TCC), IX TCC was activated as part of the US Ninth Air Force in October 1943, under Brigadier General Benjamin Giles. He was a logistics specialist, having come from the North Atlantic Wing of the Air Transport Command. By the beginning of February 1944, there were three operational wings: the 50th Wing, 52nd Wing, and 53rd Wing.

In February, command of IX TCC was given to Brigadier General Paul Williams, chosen for his experience in organizing and commanding troop carrier forces, having been the commander of XII TCC (Provisional) in the Mediterranean. He had at his command 1,176 transport planes and 1,004 crews, which suggests it was proving easier to build planes than train the necessary crewmen. Until March 1944, it proved difficult to provide enough planes for an entire regiment to train together (let alone larger formations). This was because it was essential that the crews of the C-47s be trained to undertake night flights in close formation.

In the spring of 1944, the transport units trained with four airborne divisions: the British 1st and 6th Airborne Divisions, and the American 82nd and 101st Airborne Divisions. On March 15 and 27, the units participated in 38 wing/regiment-level exercises together with the parachute divisions.

For the pilots, the most important thing was to become accustomed to transporting freight and personnel, then flying in formation, at night as well as during the day, with or without a glider in tow.

The situation was more difficult for some units than others. The 315th Group arrived in North Africa with pilots who were experienced but did not have the knowledge or the training for the airborne operations. During the previous ten months they had only been on freight transport flights, without any enemy contact. The 442nd Group was worse prepared still: they arrived from the United States having never flown in formation at night, and without having dropped a single stick of paratroopers. Fortunately, most of the other formations were very experienced.

As a general rule, the 52nd Wing worked with the 82nd Airborne, and the 53rd with the 101st. The 50th Wing, once it was operational, also worked mostly with the 101st Airborne.

The Pathfinders

In March 1944, each division created 18 Pathfinder teams, composed of one officer and nine men. The mission of these teams was to mark in advance the drop zones for the paratroopers and the landing zones for the gliders.

The IX TCC had to organize six Pathfinder teams for each troop carrier group, and each group had three planes equipped with navigation tools. In addition, No. 38 Group RAF specialized in this type of mission, with 75 percent of its planes equipped for this purpose, and all its teams trained in missions alongside the pathfinders. The Pathfinder pilots had more sophisticated equipment than that of the following waves, including more detailed maps.

The pathfinders were to drop into Normandy 30 minutes ahead of the first serial of paratroopers, in order to mark the ground. The markings for the drop zones consisted of five signal lamps arranged in a T-shape. The jump signal was given only when the plane was above the head of the T.

The pathfinders would mark gliders' landing zones with seven lamps aligned with the prevailing wind: one red, five yellow and one green. A Eureka radar beacon was also placed, this time against the prevailing wind, which emitted a series of pulses that could be detected by receivers in the Allied aircraft.

In the event that the Pathfinders were neutralized and unable to carry out their mission, the plan was that the first wave of paratroopers would jump into the area that had been planned for the drop and install beacons to be ready for the following waves.

Although the 101st Airborne possessed many of the best-trained men in the Army, there was a limit to how much training could be undertaken in nocturnal drops, since even the most benign practice resulted in injuries. This was doubly true for the glider force due to their fragile Waco and Horsa craft.

Thus on D-Day, when the 101st and its pilots faced not only darkness, but unexpected cloud cover and fog, plus German AA fire streaming up from the ground, it became a novel experience for nearly all of the participants.

Exercise *Eagle*

Toward the end of April it was decided that the 101st Airborne, which hadn't yet been engaged in combat, should take part in a large maneuver with the 50th and 53rd Troop Carrier Wings—Exercise *Eagle*. The night chosen for the operation was May 11. The 82nd Airborne would participate alongside the 101st in a few elements of the exercise. Of the seven teams of Pathfinders, six accomplished their mission. Half an hour behind the Pathfinders, 6,000 paratroopers of the 101st Airborne arrived above the drop zone (DZ), on board 432 planes, divided into 10 waves. The aircraft maintained formation as they approached the objective and for the most part the paratroopers executed their jumps well, although 500 were injured, with a number of these then unable to take part in the jump on D-Day. Two waves of gliders arrived at dawn.

A squadron of C-47s in flight over the sea. This photograph shows an excellent example of close-formation flying. It was much more difficult to maintain formations at night. (NARA)

An engine being loaded onto a C-47. Even though they had large doors, the C-47s were not well-suited to freight transport, and could only be loaded with heavy equipment using forklifts. (NARA)

Three views of a British wicker hamper used for transporting food supplies and tested by the Americans of the 490th Quartermaster Depot and the 101st Airborne Division. The basket was carefully strapped before being attached to a parachute. It didn't take up much room in the fuselage of the C-47 and moved easily along rollers installed in the floor. The basket is attached to a parachute by a carabiner, ready to be thrown from the aircraft. (NARA)

Supplying the Airborne

Aside from the glider missions, the initial wave of paratroopers included a number of separate equipment bundles dropped from aircraft, mainly containing arms such as machine guns and bazookas, plus medical supplies and ammunition.

As the fighting intensified on D-Day, so did the hunt for equipment bundles, though many fell among the Germans, and even more were claimed by the flooded marshes behind Utah Beach. At daylight, the large number of parachutes seen floating in the marshes were interpreted by some as the watery graves of paratroopers, but were more likely the sign of lost equipment bundles.

One paratrooper, while descending to earth, witnessed a gigantic explosion nearby and thought a plane had been hit. He later realized it had been a bundle full of mines hit by AA fire.

The American Plan

The American airborne divisions remained under the direct authority of the US First Army until their landing in France: command would then be transferred to General J. Lawton Collins' VII Corps. This corps' mission was to land at the base of the Cotentin peninsula, on Utah Beach, with the aim of cutting off the peninsula, then capturing the port of Cherbourg at its northern tip, which was essential to the Allied plan.

The primary role of the airborne divisions was to prevent German reinforcements reaching Utah Beach and the surrounding area, while at the same time seizing certain points to allow for a breakout from the beachhead. In the initial plan, the 101st Airborne was to jump southeast of Sainte-Mère-Église, destroy the bridges near Carentan, and seize those over the Douve at Pont-l'Abbé and Beuzeville-la-Bastille. The 82nd Airborne would land near Saint-Sauveur-le-Viscomte, further west in the Cotentin.

At the end of May, Allied intelligence discovered that the German 91. Luftlande Infanterie Division had been transferred to the Cotentin peninsula, rendering the jump in the sector of Saint-Sauveur completely impossible. As a result, 82nd Division was for the most part dropped on either side of the Merderet River, near Saint-Mère-Église. The 101st's role was also revised; it would now secure the routes that led inland from Utah Beach, and seize the bridges over the Douve.

The Final Developments

During their first planning conferences, the officers of the airborne troops and transport units determined the best drop zones, as well as the number of aircraft necessary to transport the troops.

Finding landing zones for the gliders was the more difficult task due to the nature of the terrain: the *bocage* countryside of Normandy was not suited for landing aircraft, as the fields were small and bordered by large, solid hedgerows. An in-depth study of aerial photographs revealed that the land initially chosen was not sufficient for all the gliders. Other landing zones had to be found, a tricky task that necessitated further meetings.

As these meetings continued, the planners discovered that a book published by a Czech officer attached to the free French forces contained a map showing, with perhaps a sense of premonition, sectors where the Allied airborne forces could land in Normandy. An investigation established that the book was not the result of a leak within the general staff and the censor decided to leave it on the market so as not to arouse the suspicions of German agents in England. However, a short time before the landings, new aerial photographs showed that the fields chosen for the operations were now full of large wooden stakes—Rommel's famous "asparagus." Was this a consequence of the publication of the book? It was more likely a mere coincidence, as Rommel had decided to place as many stakes as possible in all open spaces, to prevent gliders from landing. In anticipation of airborne invasion, the Germans had also flooded wide areas behind their coastal defenses, though unfortunately for the paratroopers, these were not always visible to Allied air reconnaissance.

In Profile: Waco CG-4 Glider

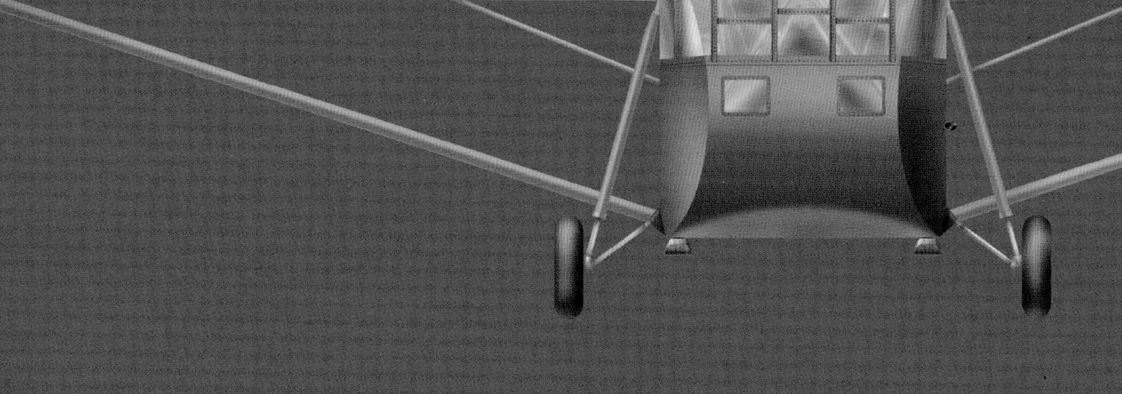

A Waco from the front, showing the lights on its wings that enabled night landings.

A CG-4 in profile: The cockpit tilted up to enable the loading of troops and equipment—Jeep, trailer, or light howitzer—onto the glider.

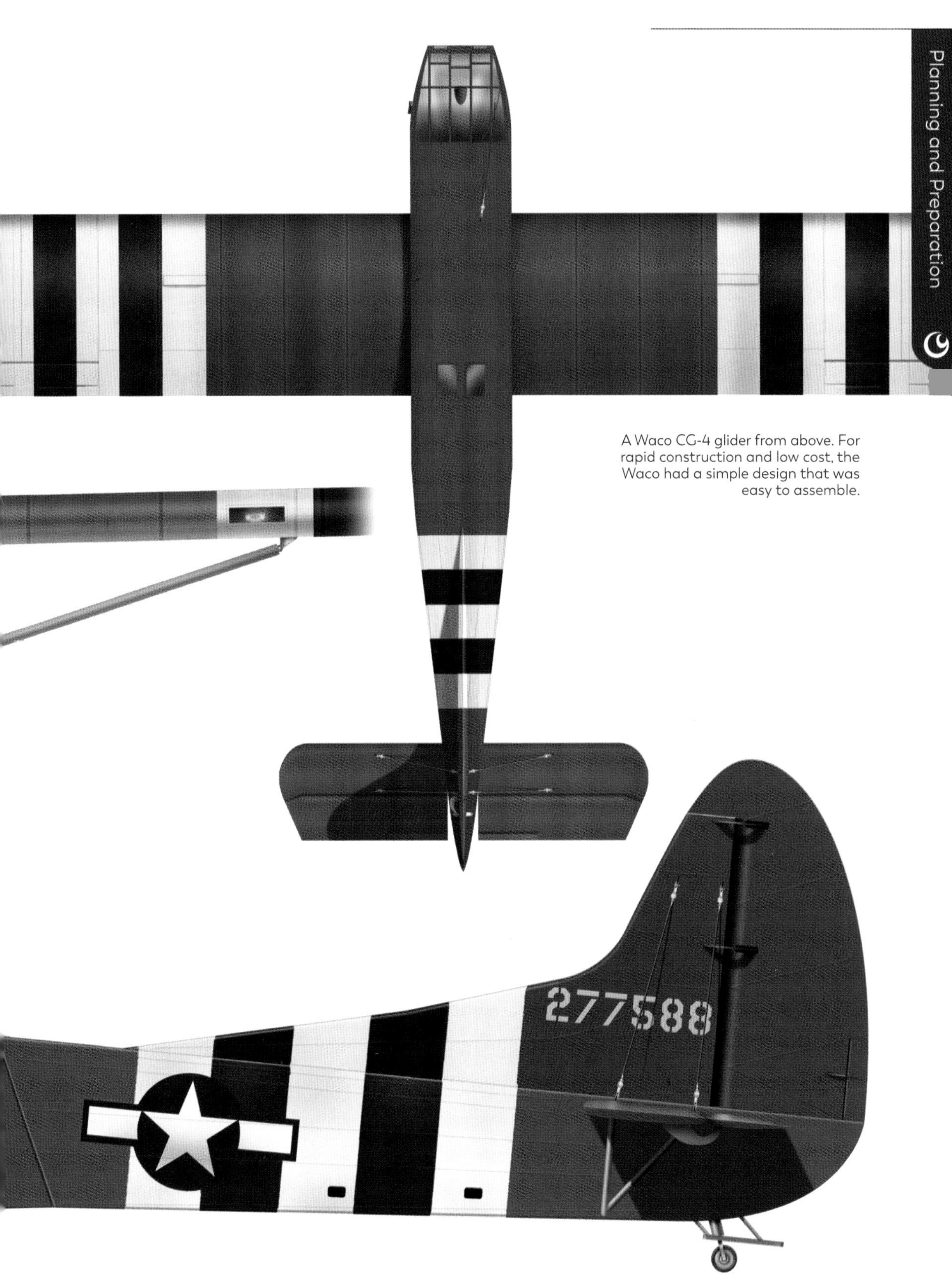

A Waco CG-4 glider from above. For rapid construction and low cost, the Waco had a simple design that was easy to assemble.

General Eisenhower speaking to First Lieutenant Wallace C. Strobel and the men of E Company, 502nd PIR. The "23" Strobel he is wearing means that he will be boarding the C-47 no. 23 of the 438th TCG. (NARA)

A C-47 Skytrain takes off, towing a Horsa glider. These British gliders were used by the Americans to transport the heavy materiel that the Waco couldn't carry. (NARA)

A mission involving C-47s towing Waco gliders. It was probably a mission undertaken by the 82nd Airborne on June 7, 1944—Galvenston or Hackensack. (NARA)

Airborne Invasion

Two main operations transported American paratroopers to Normandy as part of Operation *Overlord. Albany* was the transportation and drop of paratroopers of the 101st Airborne, and *Boston* transported the 82nd Airborne Division an hour later. Each mission consisted of three regiments, each transported in three or four waves of C-47s, consisting of 36, 45, or 54 planes—a total of 10 waves, and 432 planes. Each aircraft carried a "stick" of 15–18 men and was individually numbered within its serial. This number was written in chalk on the fuselage, ensuring that the paratroopers were at no risk of getting onto the wrong aircraft for takeoff in England.

There were three drop zones for the 101st Airborne Division on June 6: A, C, and D—Drop Zone B had been abandoned on May 27 due to the discovery of the presence of the 91. Luftlande Infanterie Division in the center of the Contentin peninsula. The serials were preceded by a wave of Pathfinders. Three Pathfinder crews were allocated to each DZ, equipped with Eureka beacons—radar transponders that allowed the following planes to spot them in the night. The serials then approached the drop zones at intervals of six minutes.

Able Mabel was a Horsa glider painted in American colors, and is photographed here during the afternoon of June 6, as in the background several C-47s take to the air in V formations. (NARA)

The First Difficulties

The first aircraft took off on June 5 at 2230hrs. Lights were kept as low as possible, so it was difficult to see the other aircraft.

To try to maintain the element of surprise, and to avoid overflying their own fleet, the formations would approach the Normandy coast from the west, at low altitude (about 150 meters) to evade German radar. A ship equipped with a Eureka beacon indicated where they should turn toward the Cotentin peninsula, passing between the islands of Alderney and Guernsey, which were at that time occupied by the Germans. The aircraft made landfall over the French coast at Portbail.

The flight over the English Channel went well, but the pilots encountered problems almost as soon as they arrived over the French coast, which was covered in an unexpected cloudbank at exactly the same altitude as the planes. There was also heavy fog at ground level. The winds were strong and German flak units were soon active, which led to many of the formations breaking up. The weaknesses of such a large attack, undertaken at night, were being quickly demonstrated and the paratroopers would be jumping out over enemy territory in extremely adverse conditions.

Drop Zone A

The weather had not yet deteriorated when the formations reached DZ A, meaning the jump of the paratroopers of 2nd Battalion, 502nd PIR was compact and neat, but due to problems with navigation and the Eureka beacons, almost all of the men jumped in the wrong place. Lieutenant Colonel Steve A. Chappuis, commander of the 502nd PIR, found himself almost alone on the designated drop zone. Even so, he led his stick to the objective, a coastal battery, which he found had been already abandoned by its garrison following an air raid.

The remainder of 502nd PIR jumped well, and 70 of 80 sticks ended up more or less around the drop zone, although this had been set up in the wrong place by the Pathfinders, near the beach. The commander of 1st Battalion, Lieutenant Colonel Patrick J. Cassidy, gathered a few dozen men and seized Saint-Martin-de-Varreville at around 0630hrs. Robert Cole, commander of 3rd Battalion, captured Utah Beach's Exit 3 at around 0730hrs. They held the position until the 4th Infantry Division landed on the beach and moved inland.

Three men of a glider regiment walk to their glider between two rows of Horsas heading out on Operation *Keokuk*. (NARA)

In Profile:
Captured French Tanks in German Use

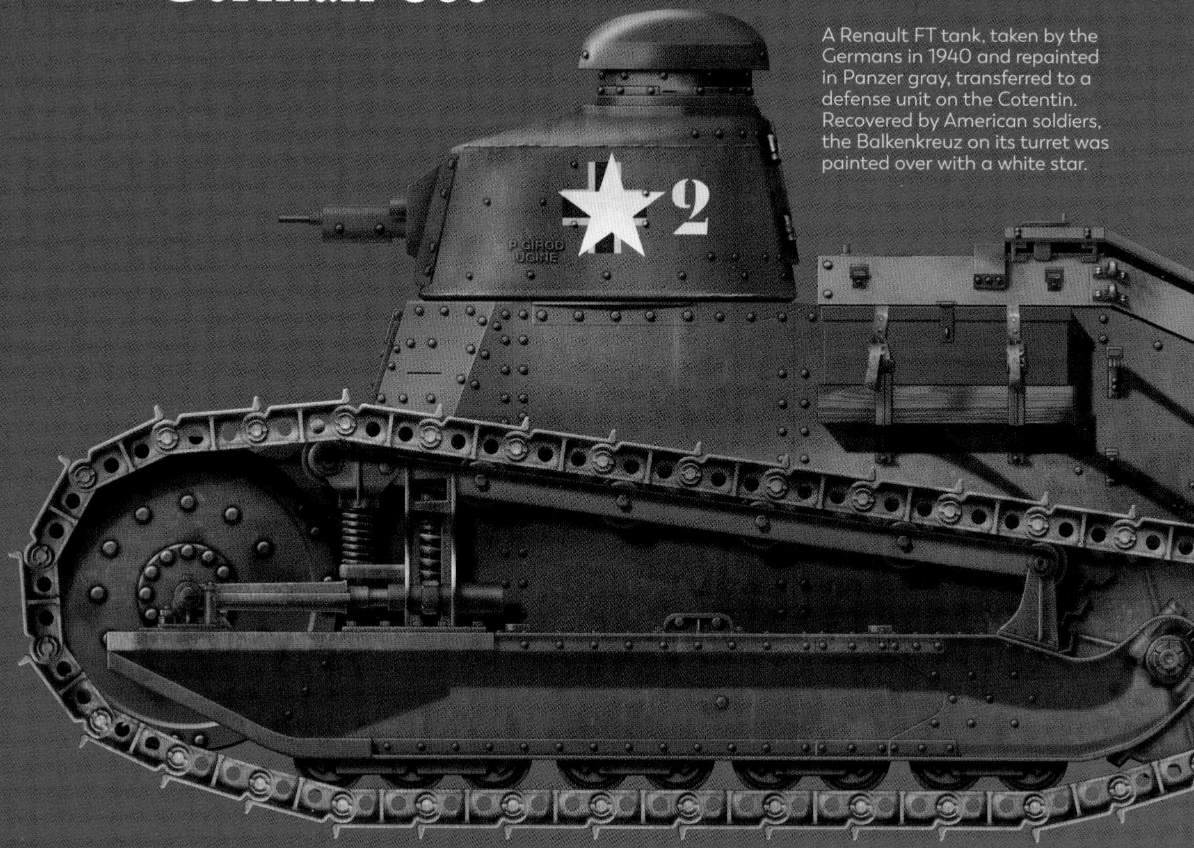

A Renault FT tank, taken by the Germans in 1940 and repainted in Panzer gray, transferred to a defense unit on the Cotentin. Recovered by American soldiers, the Balkenkreuz on its turret was painted over with a white star.

After the fall of France in 1940, the Germans inherited a wealth of captured armored vehicles; however, by 1944, rapid advances in tank design had rendered the early French designs obsolete. In Normandy the Germans organized early French models into a special battalion—Panzer-Ersatz Abteilung 100—for the purpose of training new tank crews. Given potential security functions, they also upgraded most of the vehicles with radios and improved optical sights.

At the time of the Allied invasion, before regular panzer divisions could reach the front, Pz. Ersatz Abt. 100—attached to the 91st Luftlande Division—was the only German armored unit on the Cotentin. The unit nevertheless gave the Americans a challenge, as lightly armed paratroopers were the only type of enemy they could really face, the paras only able to knock out the vehicles in close-quarters combat or with the occasional AT gun retrieved from a glider.

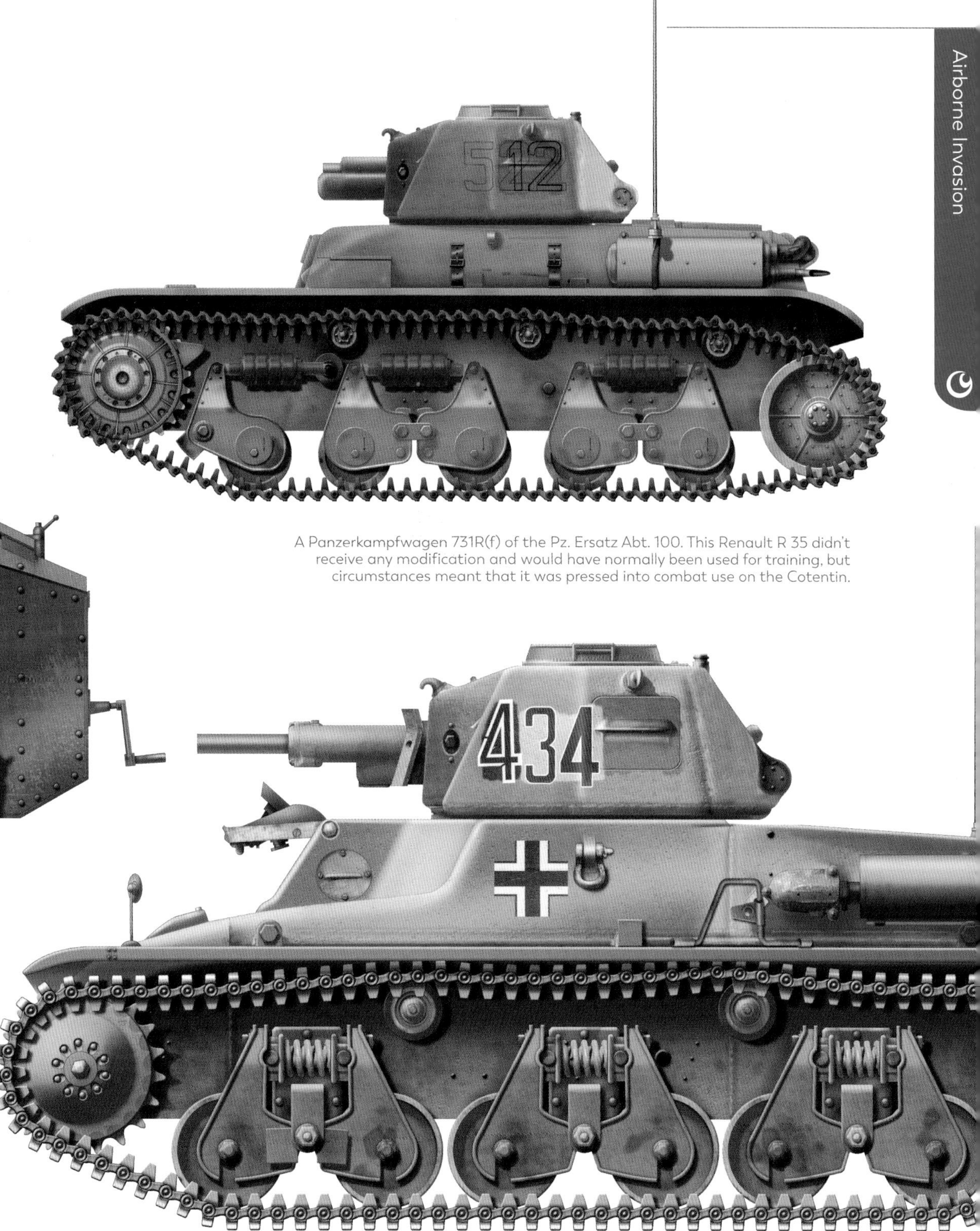

A Panzerkampfwagen 731R(f) of the Pz. Ersatz Abt. 100. This Renault R 35 didn't receive any modification and would have normally been used for training, but circumstances meant that it was pressed into combat use on the Cotentin.

A pre-war Hotchkiss tank, renamed Panzerkampfwagen 39-H 735(f), used by Panzer-Ersatz Abteilung 100 on the Cotentin. In the early days of the invasion the U.S. paratroopers came up against these dated tanks.

Horsas painted in British colors photographed by a correspondent of the USAAF. The shot likely dates to when the soldiers were training—the Horsas used by the Americans on D-Day were marked with white stars. (NARA)

The divisional artillery suffered the worst jump, and were only able to recover a single 75mm howitzer, all the others having landed much too far north, where they were captured by the Germans along with their operators. Some were found 32 km north of the designated drop zone.

A Troubled Jump at Drop Zone C

The second wave, made up of the 506th Parachute Infantry Regiment, jumped over DZ C, west of the hamlet of Sainte-Marie-du-Mont. These men had a harder time of it, due not only to the clouds but also because of increased ground fire as the flak units were now alerted to their presence by the first serial. The flak was such that three aircraft were shot down. The C-47 flown by 2nd Lieutenant Muir, 439th Troup Carrier Group, burst into flames after it was hit. Muir stayed at the controls, ensuring the stick could jump over the assigned area. He then tried to crash-land the aircraft to save his crew, and was posthumously decorated with the Distinguished Service Cross (DSC).

Two of the three sticks of 1st Battalion, 506th PIR, landed in the drop zone, which allowed the regimental commander, Lieutenant Colonel Robert F. Sink, to regroup the regiment easily.

In Profile:
General Maxwell D. Taylor

Born in 1901 and raised in Missouri, Maxwell Taylor graduated from West Point in 1922 and specialized in artillery. During the interwar years he served with a number of commands, often abroad, where he demonstrated an impressive ability with languages.

After Pearl Harbor he was named chief of staff of the new 82nd Airborne Division and then became its chief of artillery. Following the chaotic combats of the 82nd in Sicily he was dispatched on a daring, undercover mission to Rome to negotiate a possible airborne coup d'etat. Engines were already revving on 82nd AB airfields when Taylor signaled that it was a trap, and that German troops were already in the capital.

After General Bill Lee suffered a heart attack, Taylor took over command of the 101st Airborne, and was among the first troopers to drop into Normandy. He hastily assembled a group of some 30 paras around him, while the discovery that most of them were fellow officers caused him to quip, "Never have so few been commanded by so many."

He went on to lead the 101st in Market Garden, though missed the opening stage of the Battle of the Bulge while on leave. After the war Taylor's career was marked by controversy as he differed with Ike on military issues during the 1950s, became Chairman of the Joint Chiefs under Kennedy, and then Ambassador to South Vietnam in 1965. He died in 1987 after a long illness at the age of 85.

The 3rd Battalion, 501st PIR, also jumped onto DZ C. The men were widely dispersed but the commanding officer of the 101st, Major General Maxwell D. Taylor, eventually succeeded in regrouping the equivalent of a company, and set off toward Utah Beach to seize the Pouppeville exit, which he did at 0600hrs. The battle against Grenadier Regiment 1058 was tough, but the exit was in American hands by the time the 4th Infantry Division arrived.

The 2nd Battalion jumped too far west, close to Sainte-Mère-Église, which was in the zone designated for the 82nd Airborne. Some of the scattered men remained fighting with the 82nd for days. A number of others nevertheless succeeded in regrouping at Foucarville, then advanced to one of the exits at Utah Beach, arriving there in the afternoon, by which time it was already under the control of the 4th Infantry Division.

Massacre at Drop Zone D

The planes destined for DZ D were attacked violently by flak batteries, with six aircraft sustaining hits. Despite this, 94 of 132 sticks landed on or around the DZ. It was a good result, but the Germans had suspected the area might be attacked by paratroopers and had emplaced a large number of machine guns in the area, which inflicted heavy losses on the Americans. Two of three battalion commanders were killed before they touched the ground.

On board a C-47, these paratroopers—who have carefully darkened their faces—read their mail. (NARA)

Above: Unassembled CG-4 Wacos as they were delivered to American bases in England in preparation for D-Day. (NARA)

Only Lt. Colonel Robert A. Ballard survived. He gathered around 250 survivors and directed them toward the bridges over the Douve near Saint-Côme-du-Mont. He did not try to seize them due to the resistance of Grenadier Regiment 1058. Another group of paratroopers were pinned down in the same fashion.

The commander of the 501st PIR, Colonel Howard Johnson, captured his first objective, the battery at la Barquette, around 0400hrs, but could not take the village of Saint-Côme-du-Mont, nor meet up with Ballard. Captain Charles G. Shettle, 506th PIR, however, put together a platoon and succeeded in capturing two footbridges over the Douve.

The Battle of Sainte-Marie-du-Mont

On the morning of June 6, elements of E Company, 1st Battalion 506th, assaulted a German battery near Brécourt Manor, overrunning the position and destroying four guns. Shortly afterwards Colonel Sink learned that there was another battery at Holdy Manor, between his command post and Sainte-Marie-du-Mont. An attempt to take it had failed and 70 paratroopers were pinned down by German fire. A force of 60 more paras led by Captains Patch and Raudstein managed to surround the manor. The combined force was then able to seize Sainte-Marie-du-Mont. Sink sent four Jeeps to Holdy Manor in the hopes of acquiring the German guns for use by the 101st. However the 502nd PIR men who had been left to hold the position destroyed three of the four pieces before Sink's men could get there.

By the evening of June 6, General Taylor, helped by his artillery commander, Brigadier General Anthony McAuliffe, had succeeded in making contact with around 2,500 of his 6,600 paratroopers. Most of them were found in the vicinity of the command post of 506th PIR at Culloville. Their defensive line moved to the west of Saint-Germain-de-Varreville and a reserve was placed at Blosville. The bridges over the Douve could not yet be taken, and became the principal objective for the next day, June 7.

A famous photograph of a 101st Airborne paratrooper climbing into his C-47 on the night of June 5/6. In practice, these heavily laden men usually needed a comrade behind and above them to help push and pull them into the aircraft. (NARA)

Operation *Chicago*

Operation *Chicago* was crucial to the success of the larger operation as it provided the paratroopers with the heavier weaponry they would need but could not carry themselves. Fifty-two C-47 Skytrains of the 434th TCG took off from Aldermaston towing Waco gliders, releasing them to land at Landing Zone E, just before dawn and two hours before the seaborne landings commenced. The gliders carried men as well as equipment, including a surgical team of the 326th Airborne Medical Company, an antitank squad of the 327th Glider Infantry Regiment, the communications company of the 101st Airborne, and various elements of the 326th Engineer Battalion. At the last minute, the Assistant Division Commander of the 101st, Brigadier General Don F. Pratt, also took a place on a glider. He was charged with taking command of the division's units arriving by ship.

Between them, 44 gliders carried 16 57mm antitank guns as well as the gunners of A and B Batteries from the 81st Airborne Antiaircraft Battalion. Despite their name, these batteries were not antiaircraft—Batteries D, E, and F, which *were* antiaircraft and armed with 12.7mm machine guns, landed with 4th Infantry Division on Utah Beach. The other equipment carried included 25 Jeeps; one bulldozer, 2.5 tons of munitions, and over ten

A briefing before departure in a photo taken prior to D-Day. (NARA)

In Profile:
Operation *Chicago*—Serial 27

June 6, 1944—0400hrs

To transport the elements of 101st Airborne for Operation *Chicago*, the 434th Troop Carrier Group sent 52 C-47s, each towing a Waco glider, over the English Channel in the predawn hours of June 6. They arrived above the landing zones at 0400hrs on June 6. Only one was shot down—number 51.

Under each C-47-Waco combination shown at right is the name of the pilot.

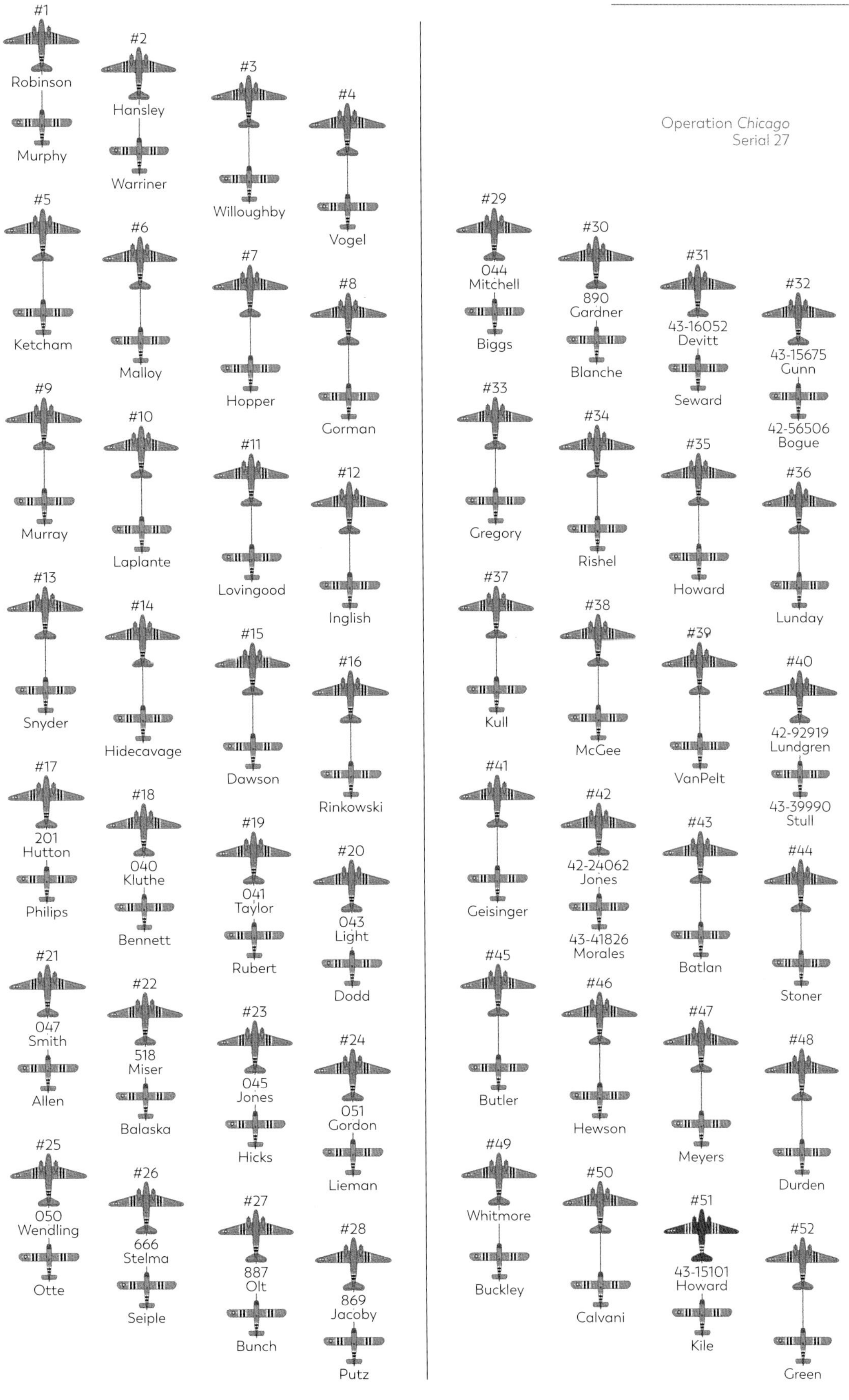

#1
Robinson
Murphy
#2
Hansley
Warriner
#3
Willoughby
#4
Vogel
#5
Ketcham
#6
Malloy
#7
Hopper
#8
Gorman
#9
Murray
#10
Laplante
#11
Lovingood
#12
Inglish
#13
Snyder
#14
Hidecavage
#15
Dawson
#16
Rinkowski
#17
201
Hutton
Philips
#18
040
Kluthe
Bennett
#19
041
Taylor
Rubert
#20
043
Light
Dodd
#21
047
Smith
Allen
#22
518
Miser
Balaska
#23
045
Jones
Hicks
#24
051
Gordon
Lieman
#25
050
Wendling
Otte
#26
666
Stelma
Seiple
#27
887
Olt
Bunch
#28
869
Jacoby
Putz
Operation Chicago
Serial 27
#29
044
Mitchell
Biggs
#30
890
Gardner
Blanche
#31
43-16052
Devitt
Seward
#32
43-15675
Gunn
42-56506
Bogue
#33
Gregory
#34
Rishel
#35
Howard
#36
Lunday
#37
Kull
#38
McGee
#39
VanPelt
#40
42-92919
Lundgren
43-39990
Stull
#41
Geisinger
#42
42-24062
Jones
43-41826
Morales
#43
Batlan
#44
Stoner
#45
Butler
#46
Hewson
#47
Meyers
#48
Durden
#49
Whitmore
Buckley
#50
Calvani
#51
43-15101
Howard
Kile
#52
Green

tons of equipment including a powerful SCR-499 radio emitter-receiver for the divisional command post.

The flight formation consisted of groups of four planes and gliders, 13 flights in total. The first plane took off at 0119hrs. Shortly after takeoff, the cable of the glider that carried the radio emitter broke and the Waco had to land in England. As the rest came over the Cotentin peninsula the formation flew through flak, some aircraft and gliders sustained damage, and one plane and its glider crashed into the Douve River.

At 0354hrs, 49 C-47s released their gliders above the landing zone. The fiftieth missed its target and the Waco landed south of Carentan. Once released, many of the gliders lost sight of the markers on the ground, and had to take evasive action to avoid trees, explaining why only six Wacos actually landed within the LZ, with 15 others landing at least 800 meters

A CG-4 Waco leaves England, towed by a C-47. (NARA)

On board a C-47. Unlike some of the paratroopers, these men haven't darkened their faces. This photo was probably taken before their departure. (NARA)

away. Ten others landed near the hamlet of Forges, while the remaining 18 landed much further away. Although many of the gliders were damaged or destroyed by trees, casualties were slim: five killed, 17 injured, and seven MIA. Amongst the dead, however, was Brigadier General Pratt, the highest-ranking Allied officer to die on D-Day. He was killed when the glider he was riding in—#1—skidded on landing and crashed into a hedgerow. The co-pilot of the glider was also killed.

Unloading the equipment from the damaged gliders and assembling the force was slow, but a patrol sent out to help extract the equipment and bring it safely to the command post returned at around midday with three Jeeps, six antitank guns, and 115 men. They had also captured 35 German soldiers.

That evening Operation *Keokuk* saw 32 Horsa gliders deliver 157 men (of whom the majority were medical and communications personnel), 40 vehicles, six cannons, and 19 tons of equipment to Normandy to support the military action on the ground. This lift also brought the high-powered radio emitter that had aborted its transit earlier.

With the gliders themselves used largely for equipment, the majority of the glider infantry did not actually arrive from the air, but landed on Utah Beach.

The remains of the Fighting Falcon glider in which Brigadier General Pratt was killed. The general was found in a Jeep that came loose when the glider crashed, and he died from a broken neck caused by whiplash. The corpse visible in this photograph is that of the co-pilot, 2nd Lieutenant Butler, who was impaled by a tree branch. (NARA)

A few landings ended very badly, like this one made by a Horsa glider, which left at least eight dead. The entire front part of the plane was destroyed in the crash. (NARA)

A paratrooper of the 101st Airborne: Private First Class Arnold H. Kantola, a radio operator for E Company, 502nd Parachute Infantry Regiment, and then for the 101st Airborne Signal Company. He survived the war. (NARA)

Saint-Côme-du-Mont

With hundreds of troops scattered by the jumps, the battle was permeated by confusion on both sides. The Americans had missions to complete and rendezvous to make to facilitate their tasks, while the Germans were encountering American paratroopers everywhere without knowing their numbers or exact objectives. During the first few hours of D-Day, darkness abetted the chaos on both sides. The Germans were further handicapped by the absence of general officers in the area. The only one who had been present—General Falley, commander of the 91. Luftlande Infanterie Division—was killed just after daybreak in an ambush by stray paratroopers of the 82nd Airborne Division.

On June 7, the 101st Airborne Division regrouped as best it could to renew its attacks toward Carentan, after the first mission assigned by Taylor—the capture of the bridges over the Douve—had failed the previous day. The division was still not complete, as the battalions of the glider regiments had not yet arrived at Utah Beach.

In order to take the bridges over the Douve, it was necessary to capture the village of Saint-Côme-du-Mont, at the junction of the causeway from Utah and the highway from Sainte-Mère-Église. It was heavily defended, with positions outside the village held by the III./Grenadier Regiment 1058 and elite paratroopers of the 2nd Battalion of Oberst Freidrich von der Heydte's Fallschirmjäger Regiment 6 (FJR6) positioned in the village.

The American attack was led by 1st and 2nd Battalions, 506th PIR, both of which were understrength. The advance began early in the morning and progress was slow, as the Americans faced snipers and the delaying tactics of the Germans. It took them four hours to cross the 1.5km between Culoville and Vierville. At 1100hrs, they had advanced only 1,000 meters further when they were joined by six M4 Sherman tanks from A Company, 746th Tank Battalion. This sped up the advance, but they continued to be harassed by German attacks from the rear. By the time they had progressed another kilometer, Lt. Colonel Turner, commander of 1st Battalion, had been killed by a sniper. In an attempt to disengage themselves, the paratroopers tried to clear the hedges that lined their routes, but were unsuccessful.

With the aid of a Stuart light tank, D Company managed to advance 3 kilometers to the objective, a crossroads on the highway to Saint-Côme-du-Mont, by 1830hrs. There the tank was hit and disabled by a Panzerfaust. The tank commander was killed trying to escape from the wreck and his body remained hanging out of the turret for several days, giving rise to the macabre nickname for the crossroads: Dead Man's Corner. There is now a museum at the site.

On June 8, Colonel Sink renewed his attack on a three-battalion front: the 1st Battalion, 401st GIR was on the left heading for Dead Man's Corner, aiming to meet up with the 3rd Battalion; the 3rd Battalion, 501st in the center was advancing via the hamlet of Les Droueries to the Nationale 13, the main road to Carentan; and the 506th PIR on the right was advancing from Beaumont toward Saint-Côme-du-Mont. The attack was supported by a rolling artillery barrage, provided by the 65th Armored Field Artillery Battalion, arrived from Utah Beach, which fired 2,500 rounds in the first 90 minutes of the action.

A portrait of First Lieutenant Ernest V. Gibson, 101st Airborne Division. He would survive the war and go on to serve during the Korean War. (NARA)

Despite the artillery support, the advance was still fiercely opposed, and in places the fighting became confused. The paratroopers, though exhausted, fought better than the men of the 401st GIR who had just arrived in the area. Struggling to move through the hedgerows, the 506th ended up moving along a road to its left, while the glider troops attempted to outflank German positions on the right. At 0900hrs, 3rd Battalion, 501st reached the road to Carentan. Its commander thought that the Germans had retreated, but when they arrived at the second bridge, they were met by 88mm fire and Oberstleutnant von der Heydte's paratroopers. The Germans had circled around behind the American battalion, forcing the latter to retreat and establish a defensive position not far from Dead Man's Corner.

The III./Grenadier Regiment 1058 suffered greatly during the first three days of fighting and struggled to hold together in the face of American pressure. In these conditions, and to avoid a collapse, von der Heydte ordered his troops to withdraw beyond the Douve, destroying the bridges, so that they could entrench themselves in Carentan. His 2nd and 3rd Battalions succeeded in their withdrawal; however, his 1st Battalion was caught in a paratrooper crossfire while retreating across a marsh, and nearly the entire unit was killed, wounded, or captured. The Americans were then able to enter Saint-Côme-du-Mont.

Robert Sink (NARA)

In Profile:
Lt Colonel Robert F. Sink

A North Carolina native, Robert Sink graduated near the bottom of his 1927 West Point class, and served with a number of infantry units until the outbreak of war in Europe. In 1940 he was assigned to the experimental 82nd Airborne and developed a fondness for jumping from planes. After a stint as commander of the 503rd PIR he was named commander of the 506th PIR of the 101st Airborne Division, a role he retained throughout the war.

Sink proved a daring frontline commander, popular with his men, as he jumped with them in both Normandy and Market Garden, before serving in frozen foxholes alongside them at Bastogne. On one occasion outside Carentan, Sink and his staff advanced too far and became surrounded by Germans, forced to fight their way out of the ring with assistance from nearby paras.

The recipient of three Silver Stars, Sink went on to fight in Korea as assistant commander of the 7th Infantry Division, and he finally retired in 1961 with the rank of Lieutenant General. Sink himself would have been amused to see his fame resume beyond his death in 1965, as he became vividly portrayed by actor Dale Dye in the TV series "Band of Brothers."

A famous photograph of James Flanagan (2nd Platoon, C Company, 1st Battalion, 502nd Parachute Infantry Regiment), displaying a flag seized from the enemy at Marmion Farm. (NARA)

A paratrooper of the 101st Airborne makes himself comfortable on an unfurled chute. (NARA)

A call to arms with Churchill and Eisenhower before the landings. (NARA)

In Profile:
C-47s Used by 82nd and 101st Airborne Divisions

The C-47 Skytrain was a military-modified version of the Douglas DC-3, which during the 1930s had proved to be the world's first viable commercial airliner. With a range of 1,500 miles and a speed of over 200mph, the aircraft was capable of long-range missions with considerable payload, and was used extensively in all theaters of WWII.

The C-47 differed from the DC-3 with the addition of cargo doors, tail hooks, for towing, and a heavier floor, to protect against flak. Lacking armament of its own, it depended on the protection of fighter aircraft or, as on D-Day, the cloak of darkness. Today surviving C-47 and DC-3 aircraft are best known by the name Dakota, a moniker first bestowed by the British.

A C-47 of the 92nd Troop Carrier Squadron, 439th TCG. It carried paratroopers on June 6, and towed gliders on June 7.

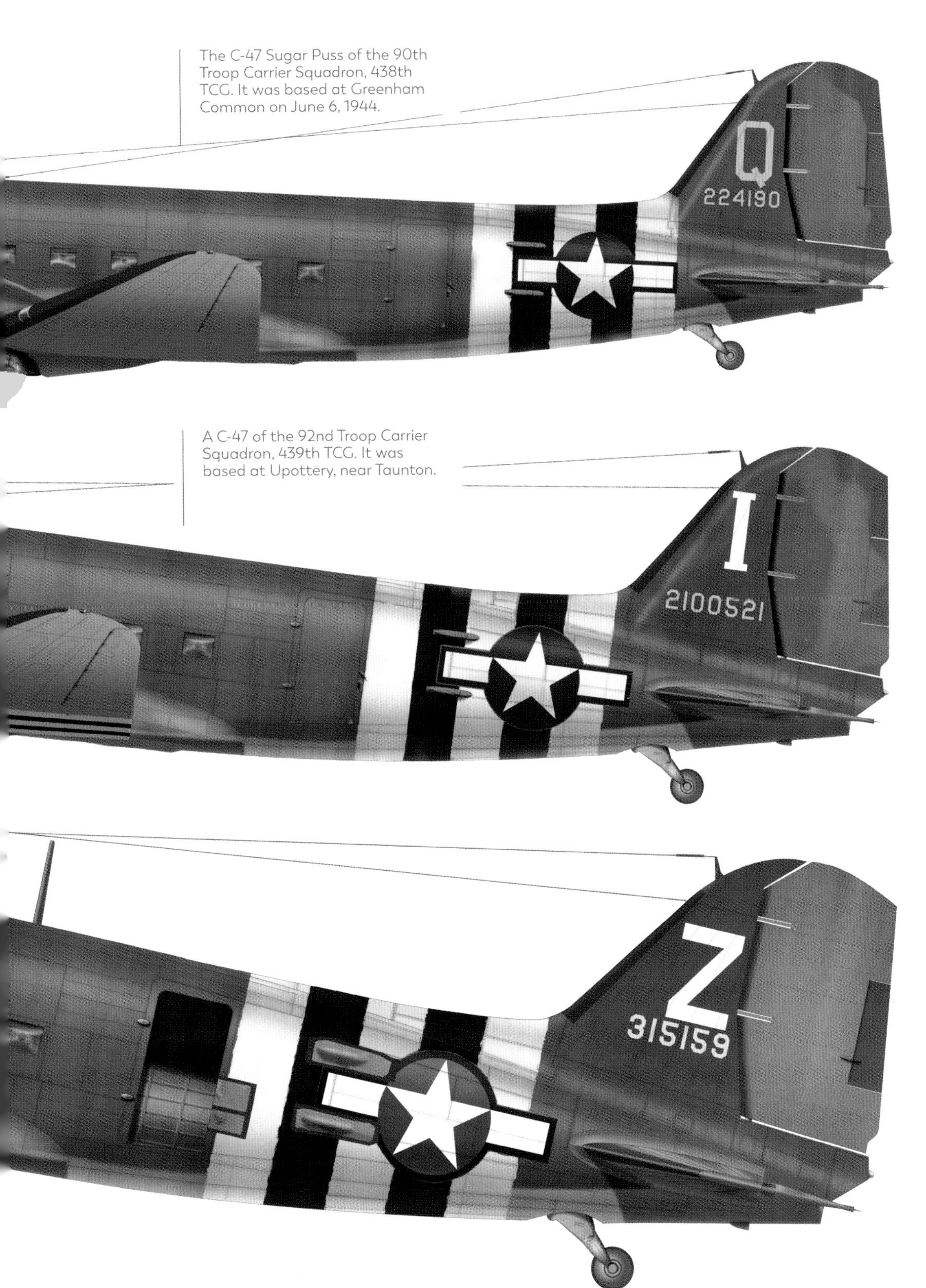

The C-47 Sugar Puss of the 90th Troop Carrier Squadron, 438th TCG. It was based at Greenham Common on June 6, 1944.

A C-47 of the 92nd Troop Carrier Squadron, 439th TCG. It was based at Upottery, near Taunton.

As can be seen in this photo, aircraft and gliders flew at very low altitudes during their missions over the Cotentin. (NARA)

Private Clarence C. Ware applies war paint to the face of Private Charles R. Plaudo. Mohawks like these were adopted by many of the 101st paratroopers to make them look, or feel, more fierce. A German veteran, however, commented that the look simply made them easier targets. (NARA)

"E" is for Easy

E Company, 506th Parachute Infantry Regiment, 101st Airborne Division—better known by its nickname "Easy Company"—is probably one of the most famous American units of World War II. This popularity is partly due to its success in battle and partly to the 1992 book written by historian Stephen E. Ambrose, but mainly it was the TV mini-series based on that book, *Band of Brothers*, produced by Tom Hanks and Steven Spielberg in 2001, that caught the public's imagination. Despite the Hollywood gloss now forever associated with the unit, it is undeniable that Easy Company's part on D-Day yielded significant results.

According to Lieutenant Lynn "Buck" Compton:

> Most members of Easy Company today, including myself, are strangely both honored and embarrassed at being singled out for all the attention we've received over the years. Really, we became famous only because Stephen Ambrose, while a history professor at the University of New Orleans, was a neighbor to Walter Gordon, who had been a corporal in E Company during the war. If Walter Gordon had been in A Company or D Company, or probably any other company for that matter, *Band of Brothers* would have been written about a different group of soldiers.[1]

But what was the exact role of this unit, whose glorification 70 years after the war's end still surprises its members?

Formation

E Company was activated as part of the 506th Parachute Infantry Regiment on July 20 1942, at Camp Toccoa (Georgia). The 506th PIR consisted of a HQ and three battalions, each of three companies: A, B, and C in the 1st; D, E, and F in the 2nd; and G, H, and I in the 3rd. E Company numbered eight officers and 132 non-commissioned officers and men, organized into three rifle platoons and an HQ section. One by one, the NCOs recruited at the beginning of the program were transferred to other units and replaced by men promoted from within the ranks of the company itself, a policy which was greatly appreciated by the men. Before airborne training, the men underwent basic training, including formation runs and night marches with full packs, so that they were all in peak physical condition. They learned how to use both Allied and German weapons, as well as studying hand-to-hand combat, urban combat tactics, trench and blockhouse attacks, sabotage (concerning bridges or artillery), communications, and, of course, jump training.

Jump training was undertaken in several phases. The men first learned how to pack a parachute, and practiced jumping from a mocked-up aircraft at a very low height (between 1.3 and 1.5 meters), so that landing properly—with bent knees—became second nature. The instructors also taught them how to place their hands on the outside edge of the doorway before jumping. The reason for this was simple: if a paratrooper could not (or would not) jump, it was almost impossible to force the terrified man to let go if he was holding onto something inside the aircraft. But with his hands on the exterior, his grip would not be enough to stop

1 Lieutenant Lynn Compton (with Marcus Brotherton), *Call of Duty, My Life before, during and after the Band of Brothers*, Berkley Caliber, 2008, p. 94.

Below: On the evening of June 5, 1944, just before the invasion was due to begin, General Eisenhower paid a visit to American paratroopers at Greenham Common. Despite their excellent training, the general staff predicted a 50 percent loss from all airborne units, and "Ike" wanted to salute the men who were about to give their lives to liberate Europe. As the aces on their helmets show, these men were from the 502nd PIR. As a kind of compensation, the men received much finer meals during the first few days of June than they had ever enjoyed before: steak, fresh bread and vegetables, ice cream, and coffee—as much as they wanted. Webster, of Easy Company, cynically remarked that they were being fattened up for the slaughterhouse. (NARA)

Paratroopers of the 101st Airborne on board a C-47. Strapped tightly to their bodies is the standard-issue equipment for paratroopers: personal armaments, ammunition, and two parachutes. A compass, three days of rations, cards, French money, a pocket torch, two fragmentation grenades, one smoke bomb, one antitank mine, explosives, a can of water, a spade, a packet of band-aids, gas mask, life vest, knife, bayonet, and two packets of cigarettes completed their survival kit. (NARA)

him from falling if one of his comrades pushed him out the door. Once they had mastered the rudiments, the men had to do a series of daily jumps from training towers 10 meters tall, then 80 meters tall—with harnesses attached. It was important that the men had experience of jumping in all conditions, and wind machines were used to simulate stormy weather. The apogee of the final phase consisted of five jumps from a C-47. After the successful completion of the last qualifying jump, the men would receive their precious certificates and the right to wear the winged Airborne insignia.

D-Day Preparation and Action

On September 15, 1943, Easy Company arrived in England with the rest of the 101st Airborne to prepare for the D-Day mission, taking part in Exercise *Tiger*, at the end of April 1944, and Exercise *Eagle*, in May. The 101st Airborne's mission for D-Day was to secure the roads that would allow the troops to move out from Utah Beach and eliminate German garrisons around the drop zone, before pushing toward the town of Carentan. The 506th PIR was assigned DZ C, near Sainte-Marie-du-Mont.

Initially planned for the night of June 4/5, the operation was postponed until the next day due to bad weather over Normandy. The men, anxious to get on with the fight, had to endure another day of waiting, and each tried to kill time however he could. Some played cards, others watched a movie, and some tried to sleep a little. As takeoff neared, they verified

A photograph of General Eisenhower's visit to the Greenham Common air base on the eve of D-Day. (NARA)

and re-verified equipment, working through the frustratingly in-depth but necessary pre-mission checks. The luckiest of the men carried only around 45 kg of equipment, while those with radios or heavy weaponry (machine guns and mortars, or parts thereof) were carrying closer to 60 kg. The men took their places in their assigned planes at 2200hrs, and took off just after 2300hrs; they jumped over Normandy between 0100 and 0130hrs. This first jump of the operation was a moment of intense stress, as Bill Guarnere recalls:

> **You prayed your parachute opened, you didn't get tangled with another trooper, you didn't land on the fires you saw burning on the ground, or get hung in a tree, or land on a German or on something that would kill you.[2]**

The drop was complicated for the division first by a cloudbank and then by antiaircraft fire, which panicked the pilots, who flew at a much higher speed than was recommended as they approached the drop zones, and at a much lower altitude. There was therefore less time for the parachutes to fully deploy, and when the paratroopers hit the ground it was often with brutal force.

To make matters worse, the aircraft transporting the Pathfinders of the 2nd Battalion had been hit, and without guidance beacons the pilots were unable to drop the men accurately onto the drop zone, with the result that some ended up as far as 18 km from their target. Moreover, the Germans had taken over part of the DZ which, combined with the flak, made the operation truly perilous. Lieutenant Richard Winters soon found himself isolated and weaponless following the loss of his leg-bag, approximately 7 km from the target. Luckily, he soon found a young soldier from A Company, and then reunited with Sgt. Carlton Lipton and two men of the 82nd Airborne. D-Day started badly for the members of Easy Company who found themselves alone in the dark, often in the wrong drop zones. The priority for

2 William "Wild Bill" Guarnere and Edward "Babe" Heffron (with Robyn Post), *Brothers in Battle, Best of Friends*, Berkley Caliber, 2007, p. 60.

Paratroopers of the 101st Airborne make their way to a C-47 in single file on an air base in the west of England. (NARA)

these men was to regroup without being detected by the German patrols. The "crickets" distributed before takeoff turned out to be very useful in avoiding mishaps amongst the nervous men. These small metal devices, made a distinctive "click-clack" noise when compressed. A paratrooper would press his cricket once and then listen for a reply from another paratrooper. The response was to press the cricket twice, making a "click-clack-click-clack" sound. If a paratrooper lost his cricket or a response was inaudible, a password system was used as a backup for "friend or foe" identification. The man who doubted the identity of his interlocutor would say the word "Flash," to which the correct response was "Thunder." Using these methods, Winters' group soon grew, incorporating members of Easy Company under the leadership of Sgt. Bill Guarnere, notably Don Malarkey, Joe Toye, Robert Wynn, and Joseph Liebgott. The detachment wasted no time in commencing its first action of the war: ambushing a group of horse-drawn German vehicles.

The mistakes made during the drop meant that many of the men were still scattered across the countryside. Lieutenant Compton found himself with paratroopers of both D Company and the 82nd Airborne, none of whom were able to agree who was in the correct DZ and who had ended up in the wrong place. This was also the case for Sgt. Talbot and the paratroopers Gordon, Eubanks, and Guth, who found themselves with the 502nd PIR near Ravenoville.

Taking Brécourt Manor

At about 0600hrs, Winters and his group met up with the staff of 2nd Battalion who, under the command of Lieutenant-Colonel Strayer, had succeeded in assembling nearly 200 men: 80 from the Battalion HQ, 90 from D Company, and six from F Company. Regrouping at the hamlet of Le Grand Chemin, 2nd Battalion found itself in a tricky position. The paratroopers had to defend the sector against German counterattacks, while at the same time try to achieve their objectives. As Lynn Compton's group swelled in numbers, Lt. Winters learned that company commander Thomas Meehan was still missing (some paratroopers reported having seen his aircraft hit by flak before the drop; others thought it had happened during landing). As the most senior officer, command of the company (which had so far only twelve men and two officers) now fell to Winters. The staff of the 2nd Battalion gave the depleted company a mission: to assault a battery of four 105 mm guns[3] near Brécourt Manor.

These guns had been pounding Utah Beach for several hours and were proving a menace to the troops trying to exit the beach on Causeway 2. As reinforcement, Winters received the young Gerald Lorraine, a member of the battalion staff who volunteered to participate in the assault. They had only two machine guns and one mortar without a base. Equipped with their meager weaponry, knowing that the target guns were connected by a network of trenches and defended by 50 men with machine guns, Winters decided to split his troops. The crews of the two Browning machine guns—Petty and Liebgott, Plesha and Hendrix—took position in a hedgerow to provide cover for the rest of the group—Winters, Lorraine, Compton, Guarnere, Malarkey, Ranney, Toye, Wynn, and Lipton—as they assaulted the trenches. Accounts of details of the Brécourt Manor assault vary, as is often the case when eyewitness accounts

3 As Easy Company would find out, the guns were actually 105 mm howitzers belonging to the 6th battery of Artillerie-Regiment 90.

Men of Fox Company, 506th PIR on board a C-47. (NARA)

are the only source of information available. According to Ambrose, and Winters' memoirs, the latter sent Compton, Guarnere and Malarkey around the first cannon, circling to the left, with grenades to provide covering fire. Compton never mentioned this in his own memoirs, asserting instead that he fell into the machine-gun nest covering the left flank while crossing the hedge.

The Germans rapidly found themselves under attack from the left flank and the rear. Profiting from this situation, Winters led the remaining men in a frontal assault, forcing the Germans to abandon the first gun of the battery. Without pity, the American paratroopers attacked the retreating men regrouping around the second gun or fleeing toward the manor. Anticipating a counterattack—since the Germans still had an advantage in terms of numbers—Winters put his men in the cover of the trenches and prepared to assault the second gun. As Lipton crawled from the tree he had climbed toward the first gun, under German fire, he encountered a young messenger from the 506th PIR command post. As the sergeant directed him, the messenger raised his head and almost immediately collapsed, a bullet in his forehead. This was the first American death of the attack, and the man wasn't even a member of Easy Company. Under the covering fire put down by the company's machine guns, Winters then led five men in an assault on the second gun, which was taken using grenades, before moving quickly on to assault the third.

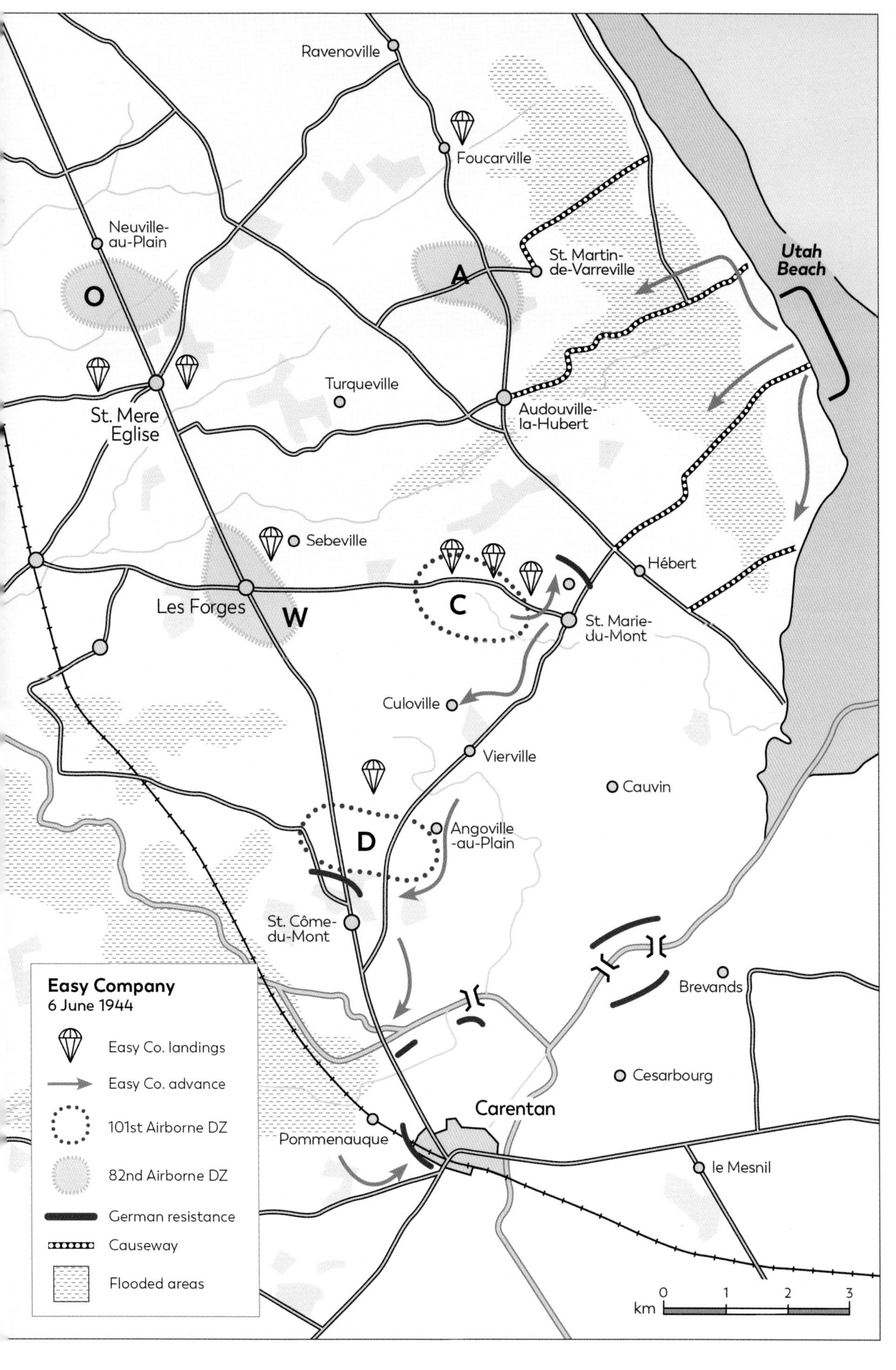

Ravenoville
Foucarville
Neuville-
au-Plain
St. Martin-
de-Varreville
Utah
Beach
O
A
Turqueville
St. Mere
Eglise
Audouville-
la-Hubert
Sebeville
Hébert
Les Forges
W
C
St. Marie-
du-Mont
Culoville
Vierville
Cauvin
D
Angoville
-au-Plain
St. Côme-
du-Mont
Brevands
Cesarbourg
Carentan
Pommenauque
le Mesnil
Easy Company
6 June 1944
Easy Co. landings
Easy Co. advance
101st Airborne DZ
82nd Airborne DZ
German resistance
Causeway
Flooded areas
0
1
2
3
km

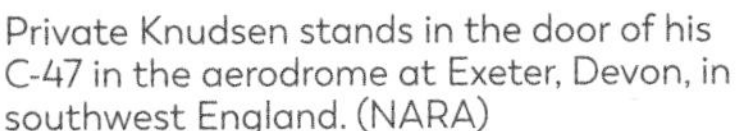

Private Knudsen stands in the door of his C-47 in the aerodrome at Exeter, Devon, in southwest England. (NARA)

A group of C-47s fly in formation. One of the planes is veering to the left. (NARA)

> **Two soldiers from another company joined us for the assault. In this attack, one of those men, Private First Class John D. Hall of A Company, was killed. We took the gun position, capturing six prisoners in the process. As the German soldiers advanced toward us down the connecting trench with their hands over their heads, they called, "No make me dead!" I sent all six prisoners back to headquarters and at the same time asked for additional ammunition and men.**[4]

As Winters searched for a way to destroy his prizes, he was joined by Captain Hester, who had brought several blocks of TNT that would allow them to destroy the first three guns with grenades (the paratroopers did not have any detonators). The assault on the last cannon was not led by Easy Company but by Lieutenant Spiers of D Company, who had arrived with a handful of men as reinforcements. Their mission completed, and coming under fire from the defenders entrenched near Brécourt Manor, the paratroopers withdrew at around 1130hrs. According to Lt. Winters' own estimations, there were still between 30 and 40 men gathered around several machine guns. The paratroopers counted 15 Germans hit and 12 prisoners taken; they had lost four men (from A, D and F Companies) and two more were injured (E Company's Wynn and a member of D Company). At the end of the afternoon, the company, of which nearly half had now been found and gathered together, returned to the manor, this time with the support of four Shermans. During the cleanup operation, a young French civilian, the son of the manor owner, was wounded by a paratrooper who mistook

4 Major Dick Winters, with Colonel Cole G. Kingseed, *Beyond Band of Brothers, The War Memoirs of Major Dick Winters*, Berkley Caliber, 2008, pp. 87–88.

William Guarnere (*left*).

In Profile:
Sergeant William "Wild Bill" Guarnere

Born in Philadelphia as the last of 10 children, Bill Guarnere enlisted in the 101st Airborne at age 19, though only after, at his mother's behest, becoming the first member of his family to graduate high school.

A member of Easy Company of the 506th PIR, by the time Guarnere made the drop into Normandy he learned a brother had died at Monte Cassino, and was anxious to even the score. In the dark early hours of D-Day, along with his platoon leader, Lt. Dick Winters, and a few other troopers, he ambushed a string of unsuspecting Germans in farm carts. Winters had wanted the men to hold their fire but Guarnere opened up, killing several, forcing the rest to surrender. A few minutes later Guarnere killed the prisoners after they tried to jump him.

After daylight on D-Day, Guarnere was in the forefront when a dozen Easy Co. men attacked a fully manned German 105mm battery. Incredibly, they destroyed all four guns, killing 15 Germans and wounding or capturing more. Afterward Guarnere said, "I'd never, ever do again what I did that morning."

Subsequently wounded in Holland, and losing a leg at Bastogne, Guarnere mustered out of the service, though he remained active in veterans' groups till his death aged 90.

The Pathfinders of the 101st Airborne prepare to board a C-47 on the night of June 5/6, 1944. (NARA)

The men's movement was constricted by the amount of equipment they were carrying. (NARA)

Above: French civilians welcome the Americans of the 101st Airborne by the water pump at Sainte-Marie-du-Mont on June 7, 1944. The village was liberated during the night by detachments of the 501st and 506th PIR, 101st Airborne, who landed in the proximity. (NARA)

him for a collaborator and shot him in the back. The company then followed the 506th PIR who secured Culoville, picking its men up in the streets in dribs and drabs, including Talbot's group, where Lieutenant Welsh had found them fighting alongside men from the 82nd Airborne.

The Battle for Carentan

On June 7, the troops of the 101st Airborne advanced toward Carentan, liberating Vierville as they passed through. The next day, Saint-Côme-du-Mont was freed and the Americans found themselves 3 km from the town, but with the task of seizing the bridges over the

A Horsa glider dismantled to allow the unloading of heavy materiel. This type of aircraft was provided to the USAAF by the British to complement their Waco gliders. (NARA)

A CG-4 Waco on the Cotentin. (NARA)

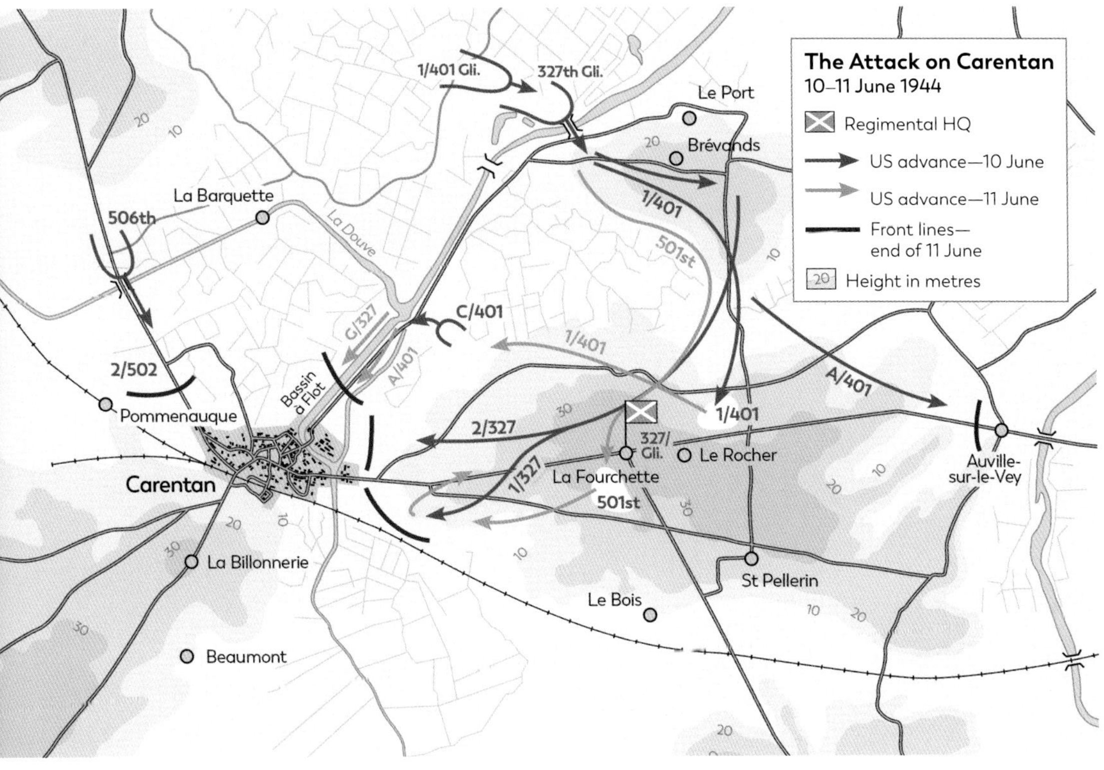

Douve still ahead of them. Eventually, the attack was planned for June 12 at 0600hrs, from three directions: the 327th Glider Infantry from the north, the 501st PIR from the northeast, and the 506th PIR would undertake a night march to approach Carentan from the southwest. The Americans who anticipated a strong resistance were mistaken—Fallschirmjäger Regiment 6, lacking munitions, had effectively evacuated the town, leaving a rearguard of only 50 men, a few mortars and a single machine gun to hold the town for as long as possible.

The 1st Platoon was designated to lead the assault, supported by the 2nd to the right, with 3rd held in reserve. Though suspicious, Welsh, leading 1st Platoon, advanced toward the entrance to the town, finding the calm unsettling. His suspicions were confirmed when, 100 meters from the town, his group was caught in the fire of a machine gun and several individual weapons. The violence of the attack caused the paratroopers to falter, and all but Welsh and the first few men of the platoon jumped down into the ditches at the side of the road. Winters rushed forward to get the men moving. Under fire he cajoled, screamed and in some instances literally kicked men in the ass to get them to leave cover and advance. The German machine gunners were distracted by Winters, allowing Welsh and his men to neutralize the position using grenades, after which the rest of the company could enter the town. They then fought house to house, the paratroopers sweeping the streets with grenades and automatic guns. According to Guarnere, the men also had to deal with German snipers:

On June 20, 1944 at Carentan, soldiers of the 101st Airborne (the paratroopers in the first row are recognizable because of their camouflaged helmets) are decorated in front of the town's population for their actions on D-Day, in the presence of General Taylor, commander of the 101st. During another ceremony in the Normandy countryside, Lt. Winters was awarded the Distinguished Service Cross for his conduct during the capture of the battery at Brécourt Manor. Compton, Guarnere, Lorraine, and Toye received the Silver Star, while Lipton, Wynn, Petty, Hendrix, Malarkey, Liebgott, and Plesha received the Bronze Star. (NARA)

> At some point, Shifty [Darrell] Powers picked off a couple snipers. When there was a sniper, you send Shifty in to take him out. Shifty was a damn good soldier in 3rd Platoon. He was from the mountains in Virginia, born and raised with a gun in his hand, not like us city slickers. He was like an Indian, lived off the ground, was very observant, was in tune to nature. He could pick out movement a mile away.[5]

As the Americans took control of the town, the German troops employed their usual tactics and bombarded their lost positions with mortars. The shells soon fell like rain in the streets, and the paratroopers had to shelter from them as best they could. Despite everything thrown at them by the Germans, the paratroopers had taken control of Carentan by 0700hrs and made their rendezvous with the units coming in from the north. Though short, the battle had nonetheless been deadly, as Compton recalls:

5 Bill Guarnere, op. cit., p. 74.

Glider pilots aboard a landing craft taking them back to England. A number of these men would be required to fly additional missions into Normandy, a fact that may account for their evident tension. (NARA)

> We walked down the main street and out the other side. It may have been half a mile, I'm not quite sure, but I'd estimate we saw a dead body every ten feet or less. Most of the bodies were pretty well mutilated, heads blown off, blood all over, that type of thing.[6]

Miraculously, only ten E Company men were injured. Among them were Sergeant Lipton, who received mortar shell fragments to the face, arm, and upper thigh, and Lieutenant Winters, who was hit in the leg by a ricochet bullet. A bazooka man, Tipper, was worst injured when both of his legs were broken.

The Defense of Carentan

The Germans weren't ready to give up on Carentan just yet—the next day, the Americans set up defensive positions several kilometers southwest of the town as the German counterattack was expected from that direction. Easy Company was on the far right of the line. As was typical in the fighting in Normandy, Easy Company was set up behind one hedgerow, and the Germans were behind the next one. After a difficult night, the men prepared to launch an attack at 0530hrs, on June 13, but the German counterattack came

6 Lynn Compton, op. cit., p. 111.

The commanders of the 101st Airborne regiments are decorated with the DSC on June 15th, 1944, in the Place de la République in Carentan. From left: John Michaeli, CO 502nd PIR (heart on his helmet); Howard Johnson, CO 501st PIR (diamond); Robert Sink, CO 506th PIR; and Bud Harper, CO 327th (here with the square of HQ in the place of the club of his unit, as he had only just replaced George Wear at the head of the GIR). (NARA)

just as they began to move out. The clash was violent, the Fallschirmjäger being supported by several armored vehicles of the 17th SS Panzergrenadier Division *Götz von Berlichingen*. In the face of the approaching German tanks and the violence of the combat, Fox Company (F Company), who held the left flank, retreated, swiftly followed by Dog (D) Company. It took an exemplary show of determination on the part of Lt. Welsh and paratrooper Private McGrath, who approached to within a few meters of the tanks to destroy one of them with a bazooka, thus halting the column in its tracks. While the Americans let loose their machine guns and mortars against the German infantry, the German tanks were hesitant to expose themselves to bazooka fire. Seeing this, F and D companies returned to their positions and forced the German infantry to withdraw. In mid-afternoon, Shermans from the 2nd Armored Division arrived to push the German troops back to their starting point.

Easy Company, which had lost nine more men, returned to Carentan at the end of the day. After a night of rest, the company was sent to the south of the town, where it carried out regular patrols until the end of the month, occasionally clashing with German troops.

The Handover

On June 29, the company was relieved and sent to a camp near Utah Beach to rest before returning to England. In less than a month, the company's numbers had dropped from 139 officers, NCOs and soldiers to just 74—a total loss of near 50 percent of its members, including 18 killed on D-Day when the plane carrying Meehan's stick was shot down.

Easy Company is often presented as a model elite unit, with the ability to tip the balance of any combat in its favor. At the least, even if Easy Company wasn't the primary factor in securing the success of the airborne operation of the 101st Airborne, it is undeniable that the unit, capable of taking an entrenched position whilst outnumbered by at least five to one, and of holding their nerve in the face of an attack by armored vehicles while their comrades retreated, played an important role.

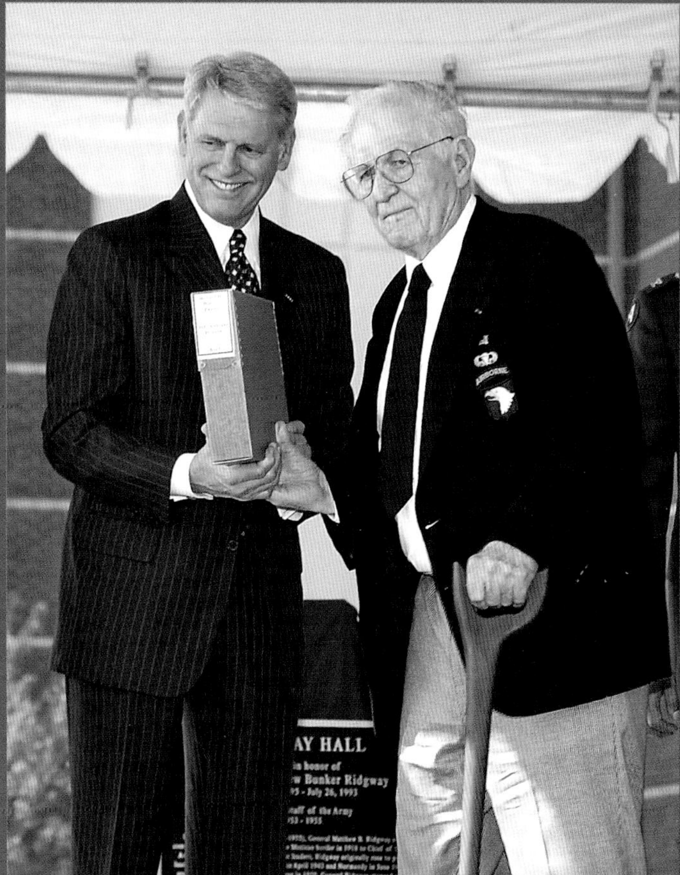

Richard Winters *(right)*

In Profile: Lieutenant Richard Winters

Born and raised in Pennsylvania's Amish country, Dick Winters had no burning desire to go to war; nevertheless, after college he volunteered for the airborne, one of the toughest jobs in WWII.

Commanding a platoon of Easy Company, 506th PIR on D-Day, Winters led the legendary attack on Brécourt Manor, in which he and a dozen paras destroyed an entire German artillery battery and its protecting platoon. Easy's commander had been killed in the airdrop so Winters took over the company, leading the attack on Carentan, and afterward Easy Co.'s gallant defense of the town against the 17th SS-PzG Division.

Winters went on to fight in Market Garden and the Battle of the Bulge, rising to XO of the 2nd Battalion and then, as a major, its acting commander.

After the war he was briefly called up for Korea and then bought a farm in Pennsylvania, where he became wealthy with innovations in animal husbandry. Awarded the DSC for his actions on D-Day, Winters found himself immortalized over time through the works of Stephen Ambrose and some of his Easy Co. companions. Winters remained personally modest and inclined to avoid the limelight, until his death from illness in 2011.

A bird's-eye view of Carentan at the time of its liberation, showing the area of the town nearest the railway station, which was destroyed by the bombing, rather than the historical center of the town by the church. The triangular "square," on the left of the photograph, is where the 101st Airborne Division's call-to-arms was held. (NARA)

The 101st in Carentan

On June 7, Eisenhower landed at Omaha Beach and ordered Lt. General Omar Bradley, commander of US First Army, to concentrate his efforts on joining the two American beachheads: V Corps would attack from Omaha west in the direction of Isigny and VII Corps from Utah would take Carentan. The latter mission was quite naturally assigned to the 101st Airborne Division which held the southern front in the Utah sector. In case it was unable to take Carentan alone, Bradley asked Major General J. Lawton Collins to make use of other available divisions. This implied changing the axis of the main effort, as the Allied strategy was to isolate the Cotentin peninsula, then seize Cherbourg—that is to say an advance toward the west then to the north, while Carentan lay to the south.

Stage 1: Take Saint-Côme-du-Mont

As already described, elements of the 101st Airborne advanced toward Saint-Côme-du-Mont early on June 8, with a three-battalion front supported by an artillery barrage. On the German side, the front was held by the reserve battalion of 7. Armee and elements of Fallschirmjäger Regiment 6 commanded by Oberstleutnant von der Heydte. These troops suffered the brunt of the American artillery, as described by von der Heydte himself:

> In the early hours of the morning of June 8, the positions of the 8th Company and the regimental command post were submitted to a violent barrage of enemy artillery that lasted around 30 minutes and caused losses.

At the end of the bombardment, the American paratroopers launched their assault. The 3rd Battalion, 501st PIR, seized Les Droueries and advanced rapidly toward the south. The 1st and 2nd Battalions, 506th PIR took up defensive positions to the east of Saint-Côme-du-Mont. Meanwhile, 3rd Battalion, 501st PIR swung around the village, supported by men of the glider regiment. The 3rd Battalion reached the highway just north of the crossroads at Beaumont in mid-morning, which provoked much anxiety on the German side. Colonel Ewell, commanding the battalion, noticed signs of withdrawal by the Germans, who appeared to be abandoning Saint-Côme-du-Mont. Von der Heydte also talked about the fighting that morning:

> At daybreak, the American assault detachments penetrated the sector held by the reserve battalion of the 7. Armee and advanced as far as Saint-Côme-du-Mont. Again, its defensive line began to disintegrate. From the command post of the regiment, I could first see individual soldiers, then whole groups fleeing Saint-Côme-du-Mont toward the west. The battalion's command post had

An American soldier smokes a cigarette during the battle for Carentan. Success at Carentan was crucial to the objectives of consolidating the American beachheads of Utah and Omaha, and creating a defensive line in preparation for the expected German counterattack. (NARA)

> changed location and we could not locate it. The noise of the battle showed that the 3rd battalion [of German paratroopers], east of Saint-Côme-du-Mont, were engaged in a violent fight.

Fallschirmjäger Regiment 6 on the verge of annihilation

It was an extremely difficult situation for the German paratroopers. They could not remain north of the Douve because they ran the risk of being surrounded, so they retreated south of the river before it was too late. Von der Heydte:

> Because of the situation, the commander of the regiment [by this he means himself] had no other choice than to retreat behind the canal of the Douve and to pursue the defense of Carentan from that point. There were not enough

A German horse-drawn cart abandoned behind the chevet of the Saint-Côme-du-Mont church. Until the 17th SS Panzergrenadier Division arrived at the front, the Germans fighting on the Cotentin were struggling due to a lack of motorized vehicles. (NARA)

Beside the Saint-Côme-du-Mont church an American officer examines a *Panzerschreck*. (NARA)

reserves to plug the breaches opened by the collapse of the reserve battalion of the 7. Armee, push back the enemy troops who were trying to get in, or stop the adverse penetration. He gave the necessary orders to the units of the regiment who fought in the neighborhood, and the two companies of the 3rd Battalion. The orders to retreat were sent to the 1st and 2nd battalions, but without having the least certainty that they were received, while the radio liaison with the 2nd Battalion was itself interrupted. Neither of the two battalions ever received the order.

The 1st Battalion, as the commander of the regiment would later learn, had been annihilated on June 7 and the head of the battalion captured; only 25 men rallied on June 9 after having broken the American lines on the marshy land along the banks of the Douve. The commander of the 2nd Battalion could no longer be reached to re-establish contact. On his own initiative, he took the decision to retreat through the American lines as far as Carentan.

It was not easy for our elements in position at Saint-Côme-du-Mont to retreat across the Douve. The majority of men had to cross by swimming to the elevated ground of the Carentan–Cherbourg railroad. Apparently, the Americans had not realized that a retreat had taken place; in any case, they only fired upon the German paratroopers crossing the Douve a little, and in a wide sweep. The railroad, which offered shelter, was not a target.

In Profile: M4 Shermans from Utah Beach

With around 50,000 built, the Sherman was the main Allied battle tank of the war, and it appeared in a number of variations. On D-Day the Duplex-Drive variant was designed to swim ashore, surrounded by a large flotation device. But that effort largely ended in tragedy when tanks were dropped into choppy water too far from the beach.

Other tanks were improvised with steel prongs to cut through hedgerows, and some were equipped with vertical intake pipes to allow fording of rivers. The Germans had succeeded in modernizing many of their tanks by giving them more powerful guns; however, the attempt to upgun the Sherman from a 75mm to a 76mm accomplished little. Or as Eisenhower groused, "Ordnance told me this 76 would take care of anything the Germans had. Now I find you can't knock out a damn thing with it."

Still, while not a match for a Panther or Tiger in a shootout, the Sherman was more mechanically reliable, and Allied crews eventually learned how to compensate for its failings. During the 101st's desperate toehold at Carentan, it was 2nd Armored Shermans coming to the rescue that helped save the integrity of the beachhead.

A Sherman M4A1 Duplex Drive, 70th Tank Battalion, as it would have appeared landing at Utah Beach on June 6, 1944.

Hurricane, an M4 of the 66th Armored Battalion, which landed at Utah Beach at the same time as the 4th US Infantry Division. It is equipped with fording equipment.

Above: A Sherman M4A1 tank of the 67th Armored Regiment, 2nd Armored Division, a unit that supported the 101st Airborne during the battle of Carentan. Below: the markings on the front of the tank can be seen close-up.

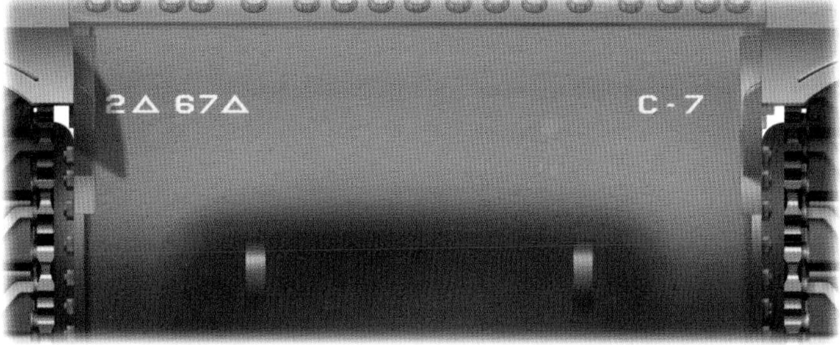

Colonel von der Heydte (left) while only a Commander. (Rights reserved)

The Battle from the American Side

Colonel Ewell, who commanded the 3rd Battalion, 501st PIR, soon realized that the Germans were retreating. He took advantage of it and tried to intercept the Germans by seizing the highway to Carentan, but his men were met with heavy fire from small arms, machine guns and antitank guns, situated in the buildings close to the first bridge. A number of 88mm shells, coming from Carentan, also began to fall among the Americans. The incoming fire meant that they could not stay on the road, so they retreated to the east. That's when, according to Ewell, a German counterattack from the north was triggered, though German testimonies describe it as being more like a breakthrough attempt than a counterattack. Ewell indicated that he repelled five German assaults; these were no doubt the paratroopers of the reserve battalion of the 7. Armee trying to reach the German lines.

In the middle of the afternoon, 1st Battalion, 401st GIR, arrived to reinforce Ewell's men. The Americans understood that the Germans were now retreating along the railroad tracks to the west of Saint-Côme-du-Mont, and tried in vain to catch them, contenting themselves instead with seizing around 40 abandoned wagons. At the same time, a patrol discovered that Saint-Côme-du-Mont was now completely free of enemy soldiers.

In the evening of June 8, the 101st Airborne held a defensive arc that extended from Chef-du-Pont to the mouth of the Douve. From west to east, the front was held by the 502nd PIR from Chef-du-Pont to Houesville, then by the 506th PIR, from either side of the Nationale 13, and finally by the 327th GIR, who held the bridges and the lock at Le Porte. The 501st PIR set up base at Vierville, acting as a divisional reserve.

The American Plan

The attack on Saint-Côme-du-Mont allowed the Americans to take the village, but they were not able to truly open up a clear route to Carentan, and there was only one they could really use—the Nationale 13. This road was swarming with German troops and was totally impractical to the west; to the east, the terrain was marshy, but was being drained and

American soldiers on the Rue Holgate in Carentan, a fire raging in the background. On the right, an ambulance belonging to Fallschirmjäger Regiment 6 has been abandoned on the roadside. (NARA)

therefore becoming a little easier to access, though it was still blocked by the Douve. The Nationale 13 crossed four bridges between Saint-Côme-du-Mont and Carentan, the second of which had already been destroyed by the Germans.

The 101st Airborne Division's plans provided for a double crossing of the Douve. The left wing, which would leave on June 10 at 0100hrs, would cross the river near Brévands. Some of the troops would join V Corps near the bridge over the Vire, southwest of Isigny, while the bulk of the troops would march southwest and take Carentan. The right wing, which would advance along the Nationale 13, would cross the four bridges, then circumvent Carentan by the west in order to seize Hill 30, a key position near the hamlet of La Billionnerie. Thanks to the flooded marshland and the Vire–Taute canal, the only escape route to the south passed right by Hill 30, so taking control of the hill would deny the Germans any chance of retreat. If the Americans could accomplish their plan, Carentan would be surrounded and the Germans would be unable to retreat.

Aerial reconnaissance showed that Carentan had been evacuated, and during one ground recon mission, some paratroopers were able to cross three of the four bridges before coming under enemy fire. The only problem, it seemed, was the fact that the second bridge had been blown up: the engineers would have to fix it before the full-scale attack could be launched.

This GI has taken up a position in a ditch, just in front of the Château de Commines. The château was the command post of German general, Erich Marcks, commander of LXXXIV Armee Korps, killed on June 12 by an Allied fighter-bomber. (NARA)

Anthony McAuliffe (NARA)

In Profile:
Brig. Gen. Anthony McAuliffe

Born in Washington, DC in 1898, Anthony McAuliffe entered a fast-track program at West Point when America joined the Great War, but his graduation in November 1918 came just after the war had ended. He subsequently held a variety of positions in the peacetime army until in World War II he was made artillery commander of the 101st Airborne.

McAuliffe jumped with the first wave of paratroopers into Normandy, though at first he had precious little artillery to command, as most of it was wrecked in glider crashes. Also falling victim to a D-Day glider crash was Brig. Gen. Don Pratt, the assistant division commander, so McAuliffe assumed Pratt's role.

The following December at Bastogne, McAuliffe earned his greatest fame as he led the 101st Airborne during the temporary absence of Maxwell Taylor. Just before Christmas when the Germans had surrounded the 101st Airborne and sent in a demand for its surrender, McAuliffe replied with the simple word: "Nuts!"

Afterward McAuliffe was named commander of the 103rd Infantry Division, and eventually ended his military career in 1956 as commander of the U.S. Army in Europe. He retired from the Army as a four-star general and enjoyed a career in business before passing away in 1975.

A Missed Attack

A little after midnight on June 10, 3rd Battalion, 502nd PIR set off for Carentan. However, when they reached the second bridge they found it had not yet been fully repaired—the engineers had had to work under enemy fire—and only one patrol continued on its journey. They crossed the canal by boat and advanced as far as the fourth bridge, which had been almost totally obstructed by a Cointet-element, an antitank obstacle, forcing the men to squeeze through in single file. They had gone hardly 50 meters beyond the bridge when a mortar shell exploded nearby, followed by rockets and machine-gun fire. Lieutenant Gehauf and his men noted before retreating that the Germans were well embedded on the embankment to the south and west, and had the advantage of height. During the morning, the battalion prepared to attack, with essential artillery support (105mm Howitzer Motor Carriage M7s) provided by the 65th Armored Field Artillery Battalion, and by the 907th

The 101st Airborne, like other airborne divisions, didn't use heavy weaponry. For the battle of Carentan, they were supported by the 4th Infantry Division, which had landed on Utah Beach on June 6. Here, artillerymen of the 4th ID are in the center of the action with a 105mm HM3 howitzer. (NARA)

An injured young French girl is treated by the Americans while her mother watches. (NARA)

Glider Field Artillery Battalion, with 75mm howitzers. The artillery fired on the ridge to the southwest of the fourth bridge.

At midday, the engineers had still not finished the second bridge. Impatient, Colonel Cole and three other men improvised a footbridge so the battalion could cross the canal—in single file—mid-afternoon. They didn't make quick progress due to an 88mm cannon firing from Carentan, but continued to advance, crouching and crawling, along the road.

After 1500hrs, the majority of the battalion had crossed the second bridge and a number of them had reached the third. It was then that the German machine guns opened fire, notably from a large farmhouse to the right but also from nearby hedgerows. The Americans threw themselves into the ditches, but a machine gun killed three men in succession so the survivors were forced to retreat. The battalion was not in good shape, pinned down and unable to maneuver, and the only way out was to get past the obstacle on the fourth bridge, under enemy fire. The German fire was not as precise as it could have been, because American artillery fired without interruption from 1600hrs to 2330hrs.

Despite this, the American advance was much reduced. G Company, at the point of the battalion managed to establish a position, with three mortars, close to the fourth bridge. I Company, which followed, was submitted to aggressive small-arms fire and, at 2330hrs, were strafed by two low-flying German fighter-bombers. The survivors—21 men and two officers out of an original 80—retreated back to the second bridge.

Toward midnight, the German fire finally ceased and H Company managed to cross the final bridge. At 0400hrs on June 11, the battalion received the order to carry on with their attack, and G Company, as well as the command group, were deployed alongside H Company. The principal position of the enemy was easy to find: a large farm, flanked by hedges, to the right of the road where the land was elevated above the swamps.

A Bayonet Charge

Concentrated fire from the American artillery was doing nothing to reduce the intensity of the German fire, so Colonel Cole ordered a bayonet charge. In preparation, the artillery fired smoke shells, and when the barrage ceased at 0615hrs, Col. Cole got up. Blowing his whistle, he led the charge. Around 250 men were supposed to follow him, but initially only 20 threw themselves forward. Major Stopka then led forward around 50 men. According to the official story, this was explained by the fact that most of the men did not receive the order to attack due to the dispersion of the troops and the chaos of battle.

Bomb craters at Carentan railway station. The force of explosions has twisted the rails up onto the roof of a train. (NARA)

On June 18, 1944, a 105mm Howitzer Motor Carriage M7, known as an M7 Priest, belonging to the 14th Armored Field Artillery Battalion, 2nd Armored Division, is driven along Rue Holgate, Carentan. (NARA)

Despite the awful disorder and the small number of attackers, the Americans reached the farm, which they found abandoned. As always, the bayonet mêlée, the great fantasy of military literature, did not happen. The paratroopers therefore seized the farm, then several machine-gun nests located on the small hill. From further south, however, the Germans were still submitting the Americans to continuous fire. The battle was far from over, as the final objective, Hill 30, was still over two kilometers away. The 3rd Battalion had suffered massive casualties, so Colonel Cole called for the 1st Battalion, 502nd PIR, to pass the 3rd and continue southwards.

The Battle from the German Perspective

As an interlude to the story of the fighting, it is interesting to look at the fighting from the German point of view. Von der Heydte indicated that for the defense of Carentan, he received two additional battalions of Osttruppen, composed of former Soviet POWs, and the rest of the reserve units of the 7. Armee, which were to be found at Isigny. As these troops were not top quality, and the American pressure was at its strongest north of Carentan, the Osttruppen were sent to the eastern sector, in the direction of Isigny. The paratroopers of Fallschirmjager Regiment 6 were divided between the defense of the bridges over the Douve and the hamlet of Pommenauque, located nearby. It was these men, therefore, that the Americans encountered.

A group of paratroopers of the 101st Airborne and a tracked Renault UE. A large number of the German armored vehicles encountered during the first days of the battle on the Cotentin were of French origin. (NARA)

Von der Heydte did not give a precise description of the fighting and he greatly downplayed the impact of the American advance on the Carentan defenses. For him, the town was difficult to hold because his troops were hindered by three (very precise) factors:

> The first is the absence of artillery, with the exception of one 88mm battery attached to the regiment;
>
> The second is the slow, but inexorable, defection of troops adjacent to the regiment …;
>
> The third is the lack of munitions, especially for the infantry's heavy arms, which are the very basis of defense.

This is not corroborated by the Americans, who reported that while German artillery was sparse, aside from occasional direct 88mm fire, their mortars were very active. The lack of munitions can be explained by the destruction of the Fallschirmjägers' ammunition depot by American aircraft. Another depot was designated, but the destruction of several bridges meant that the paratroopers had to make long detours for resupply.

Saluted by townsfolk, a Dodge WC51/52 equipped with a Reel Unit RL-26 rolls through the paved streets of Carentan. (NARA)

The Americans Threatened with Collapse

The 1st Battalion, 502nd PIR, moved up the line quickly, as they were already north of the fourth bridge when they received Colonel Cole's message. They crossed the bridge under heavy fire and deployed themselves on the ground taken by the 3rd Battalion, but did not advance further as they were dangerously understrength, having taken casualties from German mortars. Furthermore, communications between Cole and his counterpart in the 1st Battalion, Colonel Cassidy, were almost non-existent. Cole had set up his command post in the farm conquered by his men and Cassidy was in a trench to the left. The defense was absolutely uncoordinated. A group of paratroopers set themselves up approximately 150 meters in front of the American lines with a machine gun, but their position was isolated. Neither of the two colonels had the least idea of the situation on their flanks. The Americans, their backs to the river, had no rear zone and no reserves. The effect of their supporting artillery was impossible to see because of the surrounding hedges, so the artillery observers had to try to adjust the fire toward the noise.

In mid-morning, the German artillery was reinforced and their fire accelerated. The Germans then counter-attacked, crossing the orchard and threatening to overwhelm the farm's defenses, which could not be saved by the machine guns placed to its south. A little

In Profile:
German Materiel Used Against the 101st Airborne

By 1944 the Germans had gained extensive practice in the use of field artillery, unlike many of their American counterparts, who at Normandy were seeing combat for the first time. The 105mm was their standard weapon for indirect fire, while the 75mm Pak served as a mobile antitank as well as an anti-personnel gun.

The famous and fearsome 88mm was a rarity during the early stages of Normandy, yet such was its reputation that many Allied soldiers described all enemy direct fire as coming from 88s.

Mortars as well as machine guns presented the greatest danger to the 101st in the initial close-quarters fighting. Meantime, pending the arrival of panzer divisions, enemy mobility was limited to trucks and Kübelwagens. The latter was a military version of the Volkswagen, requested by Hitler from designer Ferdinand Porsche. Together with its cousin, the Schwimmwagen, it served the German Army in much the same role as the U.S. Army's Jeep.

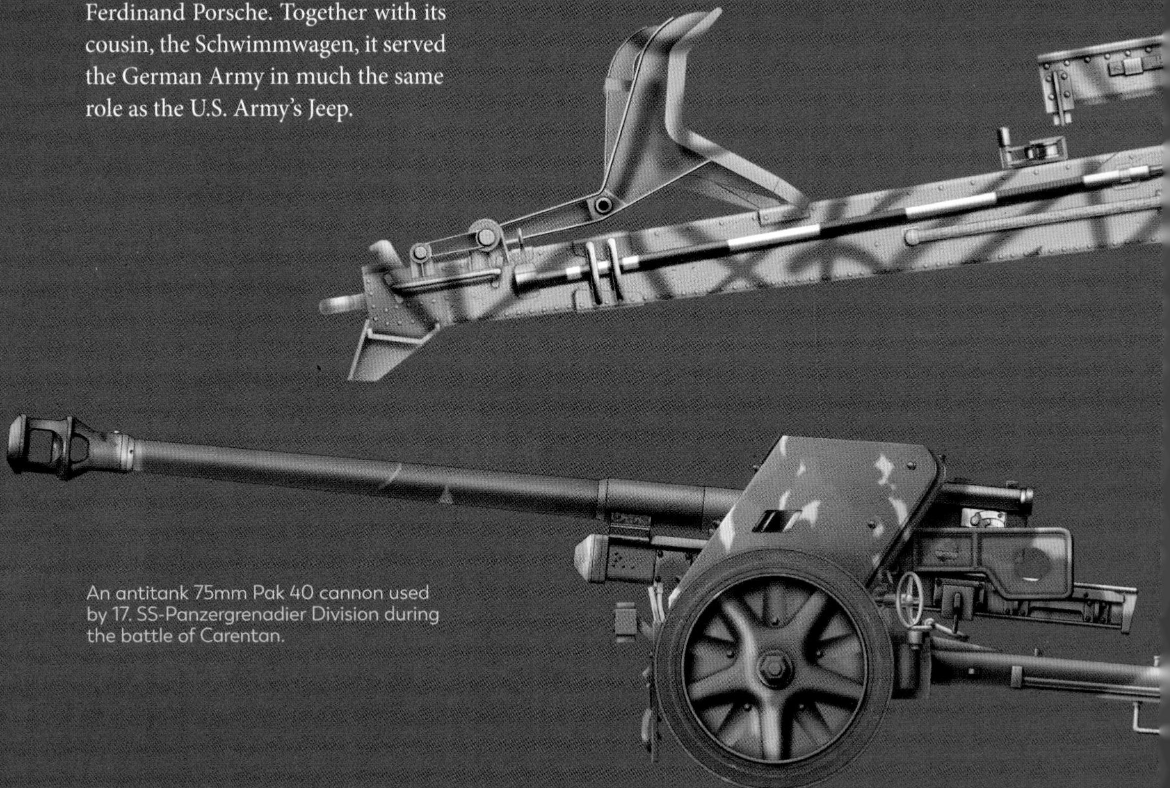

An antitank 75mm Pak 40 cannon used by 17. SS-Panzergrenadier Division during the battle of Carentan.

Above: A Kübelwagen from Oberst von der Heydte's Fallschirmjäger Regiment 6. At least one vehicle of this type was captured by the paratroopers of the 101st Airborne.

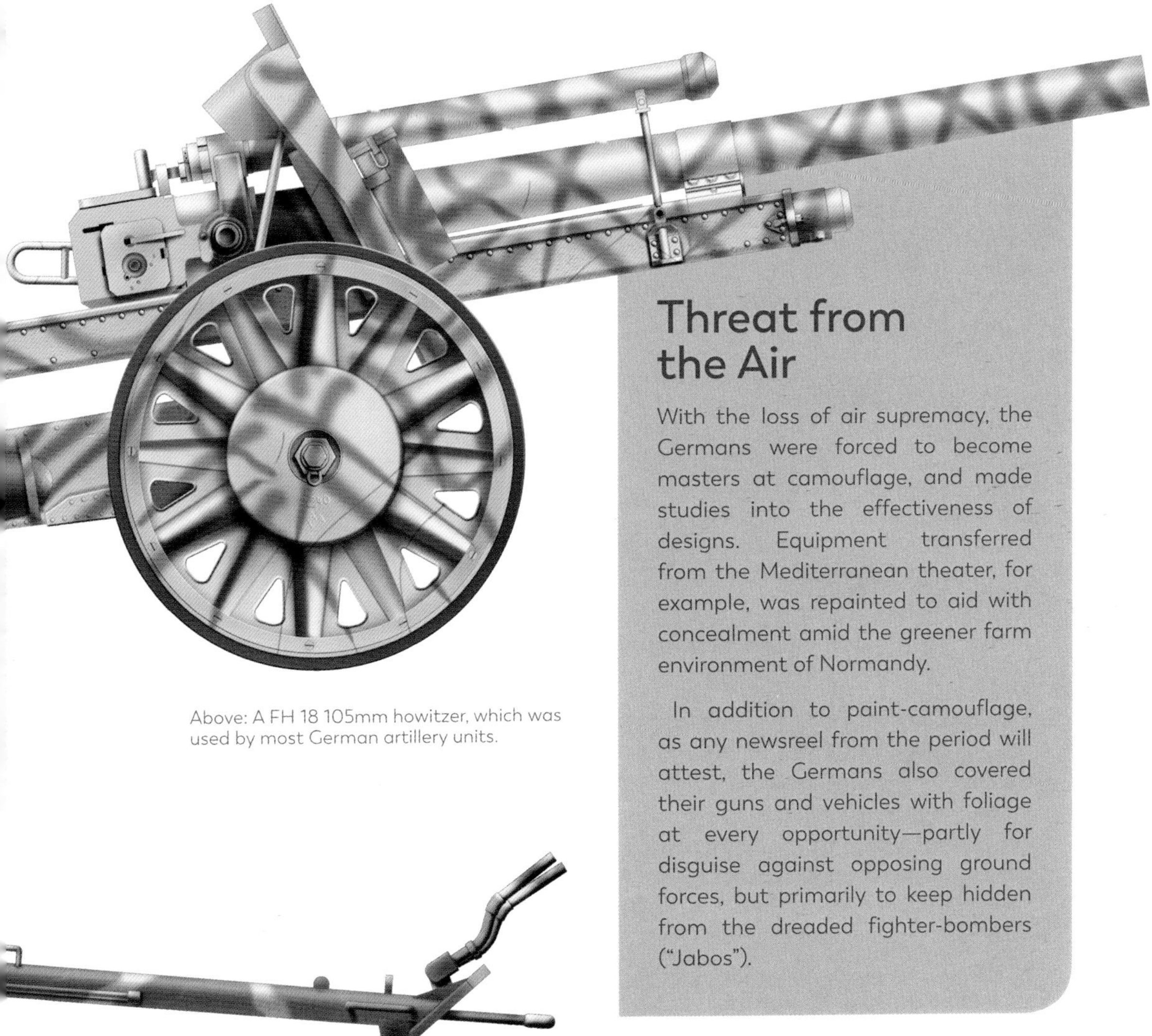

Above: A FH 18 105mm howitzer, which was used by most German artillery units.

Threat from the Air

With the loss of air supremacy, the Germans were forced to become masters at camouflage, and made studies into the effectiveness of designs. Equipment transferred from the Mediterranean theater, for example, was repainted to aid with concealment amid the greener farm environment of Normandy.

In addition to paint-camouflage, as any newsreel from the period will attest, the Germans also covered their guns and vehicles with foliage at every opportunity—partly for disguise against opposing ground forces, but primarily to keep hidden from the dreaded fighter-bombers ("Jabos").

before midday, the intensity of the attack dropped. The Americans used this reprieve to improve their defensive positions.

At midday, the regiment was informed that the Germans had asked for a truce. In fact, it was actually Brigadier General McAuliffe who had asked the Germans for a truce in order that the wounded could be evacuated. The regiment's doctor, Major Douglas Davidson, escorted by two Germans, went over to the German lines to ask the commander of Carentan for authorization to evacuate the wounded, but he was refused passage. On his return, some Germans opened fire on the American positions. Cole asked if the truce was still in force:

Carentan from above, showing several destroyed houses. (NARA)

he was answered in the affirmative, and urged not to retaliate, but his men did not care and responded to the Germans with all the firepower they could muster.

The Germans retaliated immediately and didn't stop attacking until the afternoon. There was little doubt that with the support of sufficient field artillery they would have overwhelmed the Americans, but they could only rely on their mortars. Colonel Cole, watching the battle from the second floor of the farm, thought that the line would break. At 1830hrs, he warned the regiment that he could not hold its position and should retreat. He asked for artillery support and smoke shells as cover. However, the radio was no longer working and the artillery liaison officer had to go to the artillery command post on foot. By the time he arrived the situation had improved a little, and he got confirmation that all the guns in the division were coming to support the threatened troops.

The American barrage fell just in front of the paratroopers' lines—so close, in fact, that two American soldiers were killed. The effect on the German infantry, however, was devastating, and they had no choice but to retreat. At 2000hrs, the two weary American battalions were relieved by the 2nd Battalion. It was now or never for the American troops: they had a chance to pursue the Germans and enter Carentan. Yet the 502nd PIR was in no fit state to advance—the task, therefore, fell to the 506th PIR.

In October 1944, Colonel Cole was awarded the Medal of Honor by Congress in recognition of his performance on June 11. Unfortunately, it was a posthumous honor, as Cole was killed on September 19 in the Netherlands.

The Glider Infantry in Battle

While the paratroopers were engaged in fierce combat on the Nationale 13, the 327th Glider Infantry had received their mission: cross the Douve and seize the area around Brévands.

On June 10 at 0145hrs, C Company silently crossed the river and established a small bridgehead. Shortly afterwards, the American artillery launched a violent attack, behind which the rest of the regiment crossed the Douve. By 0600hrs, the entire 327th GIR was on the left bank of the river. Brévands fell shortly thereafter.

At midday, 1st Battalion, 401st GIR (which had been attached to 327th GIR since March 1944) received the order to reconnoiter the land to the east, as far as Auville-sur-le-Vey, on the left bank of the River Vire. About 3 kilometers out, they encountered a group of German defenders, but the Americans easily gained the upper hand and put 12 machine guns out of action. They soon

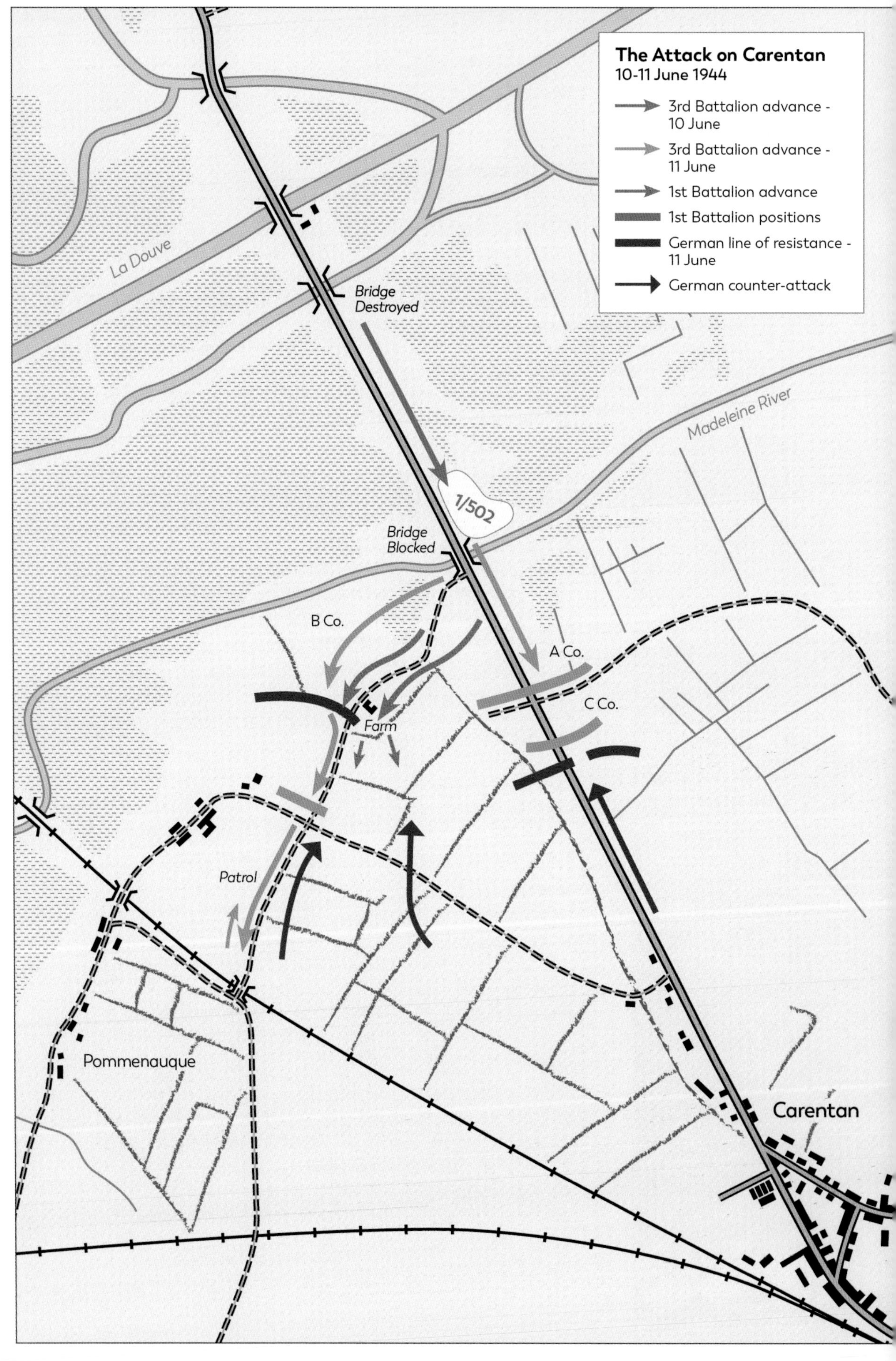

The Attack on Carentan
10-11 June 1944
3rd Battalion advance - 10 June
3rd Battalion advance - 11 June
1st Battalion advance
1st Battalion positions
German line of resistance - 11 June
German counter-attack
La Douve
Bridge Destroyed
Madeleine River
1/502
Bridge Blocked
B Co.
A Co.
C Co.
Farm
Patrol
Pommenauque
Carentan

reached Auville-sur-le-Vey, where they rendezvoused with the Reconnaissance Troop and K Company of 175th Infantry Regiment, 29th US Infantry Division, which had landed on Omaha Beach. This meeting of men, therefore, signaled the closing of the gap between Utah and Omaha. They were nevertheless still in a tenuous situation, and it was clearly necessary to blow up the lock at Carentan as quickly as possible.

The 327th GIR's mission was simple: to march rapidly to Carentan, seizing the two bridges spanning the Vire–Taute canal, one road bridge and one railroad bridge. The advance started off at a quick pace, as there were no more German soldiers between Isigny and Carentan. However, at 1800hrs, when the Americans were only 500 meters from the canal, they ran into a tirade of enemy fire, apparently coming from the houses and hedges bordering the right bank of the canal.

The three battalions reorganized themselves for the final attack: the 2nd Battalion, 327th GIR advanced north of the road, alongside the 1st Battalion, which advanced south of it. The 1st Battalion, 401st GIR, was held in reserve. At midnight, the Americans arrived at the canal. The railroad bridge had been destroyed, as had a footbridge. The troops could fire on the town and control the intact road bridge, however, and engineers were rebuilding the footbridge some distance north of the town over the canal that led to the wet dock.

The Failure of the Northern Attack

As the footbridge could be repaired, it appeared to Colonel Harper, commander of the 327th, that it would be possible to use it to surprise the Germans, especially as there was woodland separating the footbridge from the town which would mask their advance.

A CG-4 Waco in a field. (NARA)

The footbridge was repaired and at 1000hrs on June 11, two companies attacked: G Company, 327th GIR moved along the west bank of the canal, while A Company, 401st GIR progressed along the east bank. The two units advanced well through the woods, but when they were around 800 meters from the town, they were pinned down by machine-gun and mortar fire coming from the houses in the northeastern suburbs of Carentan. The artillery attempted to dislodge the Germans, without success, and the two companies were therefore forced to remain holed up in the woods for the rest of the day.

June 12th: The Americans Prepare Their Offensive

At 2000hrs, June 11, Colonel Harper was summoned to the Regimental Command Post. There, he found General Courtney Hodges, second-in-command of First Army, General Taylor, General McAuliffe, and Colonel Johnston, 501st PIR. General McAuliffe was going to be commanding the next day's attack, which would involve three regiments: the 501st and 506th PIR, and the 327th GIR.

The 501st would leave its defensive positions north of the Douve to cross the river at Brévands, where a treadway bridge had been built, and then veer off toward the southwest to meet up with the men of the 506th, who had left the Nationale 13 for Hill 30 at Billonnerie. This was where they would attack on the west flank.

A fireman attempts to extinguish a fire in a large building, while a Jeep with a soldier sitting on the hood drives past. (NARA)

Three soldiers of the 101st Airborne: Charles E. Rinehart and Charles A. West, 506th Parachute Infantry Regiment, and James V. Longane, 327th Glider Infantry Regiment pose in front of the war memorial in Carentan after its liberation. (NARA)

The capture of the town was effectively entrusted to the 327th GIR; its first two battalions would hold the canal at the side of the Isigny road. The attack itself was launched from the northeast by the 1st Battalion, 401st GIR and G Company, 327th GIR.

During the night, the American artillery raged against the town, which soon caught fire. Artillery fire from the countryside, heavy mortars, tank destroyers—even naval fire from the fleet—subjected the town to a brutal attack. Part of the town center was totally destroyed, but most of the old houses in Carentan were fortunately spared. As it turned out, the bombardment was unnecessary as the Germans had already pulled back.

Von der Heydte Moves Out

While the American generals were preparing the final assault on Carentan, Oberstleutnant von der Heydte ordered his men to abandon the town. His decision to do so was sound, if one believes his account of the event:

> On June 11, the munitions situation became so critical in the regiment that its commander used the radio to ask the paratrooper army for supplies to be sent by air, with the help of Ju-52 and He-111 aircraft. All the gun cartridges were collected so they could be used by the machine guns, so that the men could no longer defend themselves with their own weapons.

The liberation of Carentan came at a high cost to its population, as American aircraft first bombarded the town, and then German artillery responded once the paratroopers had broken in. Here, after the fighting, civilians seek to discover what is left. (NARA)

Bundesarchiv Bild 183-H26044 / o.Ang.

In Profile:
Oberstleutnant Friedrich Freiherr von der Heydte

One of the most prominent of German airborne commanders, von der Heydte (born in 1907) commanded a battalion in the invasion of Crete, and then in North Africa in the famed Ramcke Brigade. After helping to secure Rome after the fall of Sicily, von der Heydte was given command of Fallschirmjäger Regiment 6, stationed in Normandy.

It was FJR6 that provided the 101st Airborne its toughest opposition on D-Day and beyond—kind meets kind—as the German paras were dubbed "The Lions of Carentan" for their dogged defense of the key town. Bled white during the battle, FJR6 regrouped and met the 101st again two months later in Holland.

Ironically it was during the Ardennes Offensive, when the 82nd and 101st Airborne were fighting as infantry, that von der Heydte led Germany's last airborne assault. It turned into a disaster as the Fallschirmjäger were badly scattered in the night-time drop, and few were able to assemble on their objective. With panzer support failing to reach him, von der Heydte could only order a breakout, though hardly any men made it back and he was personally captured. He went on to a controversial career in postwar Germany before passing away in 1994.

A GI has a well-deserved wash at Carentan. (NARA)

During the night of the 11th, the aerial resupply was carried out by the paratrooper army in an exemplary fashion. The munitions were dropped in a field at Raids, marked by lanterns, approximately 14 km from the front.

In the morning of the 11th, at Pommenauque, the Americans managed to strengthen themselves greatly on our Main Line of Resistance. It was not possible to repel them, but their advance ceased and was continued by assault detachments.

Concerning the continual extension of our front and our heavy losses, the regiment's MLR was stretched to such a point that the commander of the regiment had no doubt that on June 12, the Americans would succeed in penetrating the lines and would then seize the town. In consequence, he refused to take the responsibility for sacrificing the rest of the regiment for the battle of Carentan and decided to evacuate the town at the end of the afternoon.

Contrary to what might have been feared, he was able to evacuate Carentan in broad daylight without interference on the part of the enemy, which seemed to be reorganizing itself at the time … The regiment, with the elements that were subordinate to it, set up a new defensive position to the southwest of Carentan. Hill 30, also southwest of the town, was the anchor point of the new position.

The commander of the regiment had warned LXXXIV Armee Korps of his decision to abandon Carentan and the army corps had approved this decision. The commander of the regiment was then greatly surprised, during the afternoon of June 11, just after the evacuation of the bulk of the regiment, to see the commander of the 17th SS Panzergrenadier Division arrive to inform him

A mass for the American soldiers in the Notre Dame church in Carentan, which survived the battle. (NARA)

> that his division would be arriving during the night to relieve the regiment in the defense of Carentan.

That was von der Heydte's account of what happened on June 11—in brief, lack of munitions and heavy losses led to the abandonment of Carentan to avoid the destruction of the regiment, while its commander (von der Heydte) had been unaware that the 17th SS Panzergrenadier Division was on its way to relieve them. However, his version of events is totally contradicted by that of General Pemsel, head of the general staff of 7. Armee:

> The premature abandonment of Carentan in the afternoon of June 11, which the commander of Fallschirmjäger Regiment 6 had decided on his own initiative, is a measure both incomprehensible and very badly considered, especially since the commander had been informed of the imminent arrival of the 17th SS Panzergrenadier Division at Carentan before making his decision, and not after, contrary to what he has written. The archives of the 7. Armee are clear: LXXXIV Armee Korps had been told on June 10 at 1300hrs, and then again on June 11 at 1145hrs, that the 17th SS Panzergrenadier Division was coming to intervene at Carentan. In addition, the head of the general staff of LXXXIV Armee Korps has declared that he was personally warned by the head of Fallschirmjäger Regiment 6 of the arrival of the SS Panzergrenadier Division on June 10.
>
> Neither the army nor the army corps gave their agreement to this unilateral decision... Because of the severe—and disastrous—battles that he had just led, the commander of the Fallschirmjäger Regiment 6 went through a grave physical and moral depression which explains his insane order ... It is only

In Profile:
German Armored Vehicles

A premise of the airborne incursion at Normandy was that lightly armed paratroopers would not have to face main-strength panzer units before heavier help could arrive from the beaches. At Carentan this margin temporarily disappeared, as the 17th SS-Panzergrenadier Division arrived to counterattack the thin para line.

Equipped with Sturmgeschütz assault guns with 75mm main armament, armored half-tracks, and a full complement of artillery, the 17th SS nearly swept the 101st paras away before 2nd AD Shermans arrived to even the odds. The destruction of a Stug at close range by a courageous Easy Co. bazooka team also gave pause to the enemy onslaught.

Though not as renowned as its more glamorous Panther and Tiger cousins, the Stug proved a mainstay for the Wehrmacht throughout the war, and in Russia some credited it as a superior weapon in an antitank role.

A Sturmgeschütz IV of 17th SS Panzergrenadier Division. This type of StuG with a Panzer IV chassis is rare, but the *Götz von Berlichingen* owned several examples.

A SdKfz 251/1 Ausf. D of the 17th SS Panzergrenadier Division during the battle of Carentan.

In liberated Carentan, GIs watch Jeeps file past. One of these is pulling an antitank cannon. (NARA)

In Carentan, some houses suffered particularly badly, the victim of bombs, or destroyed by Allied forces trying to eliminate pockets of German resistance. (NARA)

> because he previously rendered such great service and because he had to quickly re-enter service that the commander of the Fallschirmjäger Regiment 6 has not been punished and relieved of his command.

Evidently, von der Heydte's responsibility was clearly confirmed by the military hierarchy. His abandonment of Carentan, for whatever reason, would have grave consequences for the Germans.

The Americans Enter Carentan

On June 12 at 0200hrs, the 1st and 2nd Battalions of 506th PIR entered Carentan. The official story indicates that they didn't meet with significant resistance, and of course we already know the reason for this—there were few German troops left in the town. On the other hand—and this was not mentioned by von der Heydte—the 1st Battalion overwhelmed a line of German outposts and seized Hill 30, though von der Heydte himself considered this a key position in his new line of defense. The 2nd Battalion established itself to the right of the 1st Battalion.

The commander of the 506th PIR, Colonel Sink, advanced in the night with his HQ staff, following the two battalions. In the darkness, however, he got lost and ended up south of Hill 30—ahead of his own troops, inside the German lines.

A Willys Jeep of the 759th Tank Battalion. This unit of M3 light tanks landed at Utah Beach on D+10, i.e. June 16, and was attached to the 2nd Infantry Division, fighting in the St Lô area.

Another prize of battle: a Kübelwagen recovered by the men of the 101st Airborne Division. (NARA)

At 0500hrs, Col. Sink ordered the 2nd Battalion to march on Carentan to rendezvous with the air transport troops of 1st Battalion, 401st GIR. As day broke, the Germans realized that a group of Americans had passed behind their lines and began to fire furiously on them. The 1st Battalion, 506th PIR immediately made for Hill 30 to rescue Colonel Sink, but the battle raged on for several hours before they were able to reach Sink and safely extract him and his staff. During this time, the 2nd Battalion departed for Carentan, and was subjected to violent machine-gun fire from the south.

On the northeast side of Carentan, the 1st Battalion, 401st GIR left the woods at 0600hrs to attack the wet dock sector. Encountering no resistance, the battalion quickly reached the town center and rendezvoused there with the 2nd Battalion at around 0730hrs after a final exchange of fire with some German stragglers near the train station.

Some happy inhabitants of liberated Carentan, though some still look anxious as aircraft pass overhead. (NARA)

As this was happening, the left wing of the American "pincers" set out. At dawn, the 501st PIR crossed the canal and continued its advance toward Hill 30, coming from the northeast, to make their own rendezvous with the 1st Battalion, 506th PIR, at 0800hrs.

The double "pincer" maneuver therefore closed south of Carentan, though it did not trap the enemy, save for a few stragglers, as the German paratroopers had retreated the previous day. It was now essential for the Americans to hold Carentan and maintain the connection between the two Normandy footholds of Omaha and Utah.

Von der Heydte Surprised

After his orderly retreat during the day of June 11, von der Heydte believed himself to be sheltered from a new American attack before the 13th. Yet the Americans attacked on the 12th, barreling toward Hill 30, which had not yet been organized for defense. In fact, von der Heydte had withdrawn his paratroopers behind this position in order to reorganize them and had placed the Osttruppen on the front line. It was this battalion that was attacked by the 101st Airborne, and defended the hill in such a lackluster fashion that the Americans were on the verge of seizing it.

Understanding the danger he and his regiment were in, von der Heydte immediately launched a counterattack with the only resource he had, a squad of engineers, which he led into battle himself, albeit without success. It is probable that this *kampfgruppe* was the force that fought the Americans who came to extract Colonel Sink.

In Profile: American Armored Vehicles

Although the M4 Sherman comprised the ubiquitous backbone of American armor, other vehicles in Normandy provided specialized service.

The M3/M5 light tank, aptly dubbed the "Stuart" by the British, was designed as a fast, light cavalry tank, sporting only a 37mm main gun but with coaxial machine guns in the hull. Though vulnerable to enemy tanks or heavy weapons (see "Dead Man's Corner" outside Saint Côme-du-Mont), it was an excellent scouting and anti-personnel vehicle.

The same can be said for the M8 Greyhound armored car, which eschewed tracks for heavy tires, and could reach a speed of 50mph.

On the other side of the coin was the M10 Tank Destroyer, with a 76.2mm (3-inch) main gun supported by a .50-cal machine gun. Superior to most German tanks and nearly equivalent to the Panther (if not Tiger), the M-10 was further upgraded until it ended the war as the formidable M-36.

An M5A1 light tank (known as a Stuart) of the 758th Tank Battalion.

Below: An armored M8, which served as support for the 82nd Airborne Division on the Cotentin.

Below: An M10 tank destroyer of the 702nd Tank Destroyer Battalion. This unit provided support for the 4th Infantry Division as well as for the two airborne divisions.

During this time, the 17th SS Panzergrenadier Division took up position and prepared to launch its counteroffensive to retake Carentan, with a Panzergrenadier regiment, a Sturmgeschütz battalion, and the support of the majority of the divisional artillery.

Apparently, the commander of the SS division was sure of his success, as he asked von der Heydte: "After we retake Carentan, would you prefer us to continue in the direction of Isigny or veer off to the left, toward Sainte-Mère-Eglise?"

The German Counteroffensive

By the evening of June 12, the Americans had increased their hold on the southeast of the town, in the direction of Isigny, by capturing the village of Montmartin-en-Graignes. The most important sector remained the southwest route out of Carentan, principally on the Périers road, beyond Hill 30—the direction from which a German counterattack would come.

The commander of the 17th SS Panzergrenadier Division was counting on the element of surprise: he refused to allow any reconnaissance or preliminary artillery barrage, meaning that the positions of the Americans were unknown.

Supervised by several guards, German prisoners dig graves in a makeshift cemetery in Carentan. (NARA)

The assault began at 0700hrs, at the exact time the 506th PIR launched its own attack. The StuG IIIs were quite quickly stopped by antitank guns, at around 800 meters from the first houses of Carentan. At around 0900hrs, the Panzergrenadiers and von der Heydte's paratroopers engaged American troops. The FJR6 commander noted: "I had the impression that they were not organized for defense, but that they were advancing."

The battle played out from hedgerow to hedgerow, which the German paratroopers were more familiar with than the Waffen-SS, so the former advanced to within a few hundred meters of the railway line, while the Panzergrenadiers were very quickly stopped in their tracks.

The situation soon became dangerous for the 17th SS Panzergrenadier Division, as the American paratroopers—who by this time had a week's worth of experience of fighting in the bocage—succeeded in infiltrating the German lines. The commander of the SS division was therefore forced to fire on the Americans in his rear and on his flanks. According to von der Heydte, the Waffen-SS gave ground and descended into disorder. These were not seasoned troops, and the German paratroopers were forced to round up attempted fugitives, sometimes at gunpoint. By midday, the Germans had lost the battle. Carentan would not be retaken.

Von der Heydte Stopped by the Waffen-SS

The situation was even worse in the afternoon: von der Heydte ordered his troops to retreat so they could establish a more solid position, between Varimesnil and Raffoville, and placed the Panzergrenadier regiment under his orders. This withdrawal went well, but at the end of the day von der Heydte was summoned to the command post by the commander of the 17th SS Panzergrenadier Division and arrested for "cowardice in the face of the enemy," a crime punishable by death. He was interrogated for much of the night by an SS officer, and was finally released the following morning at the request of General Meindl, head of the 2nd Fallschirmjäger Korps, who was temporarily in command of LXXXIV Armee Korps following the death of General Marcks, who was fatally wounded by an Allied air attack on the road from Saint Lô to Carentan on June 12.

With the end of the battle of Carentan, Fallschirmjäger Regiment 6 was recalled from the sector. The tough German paratroopers would face their Normandy counterparts—the 101st Airborne Screaming Eagles—again, however, in the following September on Hell's Highway in the Netherlands.

The Battle from the American Perspective

According to the US Army Center of Military History, the German counterattack advanced to within 500 meters of Carentan. The 2nd Battalion, 502nd PIR, had been called upon to reinforce the right flank of the 506th PIR, which had held its position. "But the attack threatened the junction of the bridgeheads of V and VII Corps, so the First Army had decided to send armored vehicles to repel it. It was necessary to await the arrival of the tanks so that the German threat could be eliminated and the link between the two corps secured."

Paratroopers of the 101st Airborne with their "new" semi-tracked SdKfz 2 *Kettenkrad*. (NARA)

As part of their liberation it became necessary to destroy many of the French towns and villages in Normandy, either when they were defended by Germans or when the Germans counterattacked with artillery after their seizure by Americans.

The French population nevertheless welcomed the overthrow of the Wehrmacht, often assisting the GIs with medical assistance or shelter when the enemy was near. The postwar period would see assistance to the French in turn, as the Marshall Plan helped Europe to recover from its destruction.

Right: In front of a farm near Carentan, the paratroopers of the 101st Airborne are heartily welcomed by locals, who were particularly happy because the town and its surroundings were not badly damaged by the bombings. (NARA)

Elements of Combat Command A, 2nd Armored Division arrived at Carentan at 1030hrs, June 13. Two task forces were scheduled to leave at 1400hrs, one along the Carentan–Baupe road, the other along the Carentan–Périers road. It is interesting to note that von der Heydte did not allude to this and preferred instead to talk about the inexperience of the young Waffen-SS troops.

For the Germans, the loss of Carentan was a significant defeat, even though the human losses suffered were not catastrophic, thanks to von der Heydte's evacuation of the town. He was certain that if the 17th SS Panzergrenadier Division had arrived at Carentan before it had been captured, the Americans would have had much more difficulty connecting their two bridgeheads.

The participation of the 101st Airborne Division in the battle of Normandy was not limited to the capture of Carentan, though that was without doubt the most important feat of arms, strategically speaking, achieved by the division. The two American airborne divisions fought in Normandy for 33 days, before being relieved on July 8, 1944 and returning to England. In Normandy the 101st Airborne had suffered nearly 50 percent casualties—868 killed, 2,303 wounded, and 665 missing—and needed time to incorporate and train replacements. Otherwise the 101st, along with the 82nd, would stand by in case they were needed to intervene on the continent once more. They would indeed do so in less than two months, as part of Operation *Market Garden*, to clear the way for the British XXX Corps to the Rhine.

Men of the 101st Airborne packed into a landing barge for transit to a larger ship for the journey back to England, on July 8–9, 1944. (NARA)

LC

Afterword

Although the invasion of Normandy on June 6, 1944 has often been called the most daring military operation in history, the most dangerous element of D-Day itself was the employment of the airborne divisions.

No one knew for sure how strong the German defenses would be, nor whether they'd be ready for the invasion. It was conceivable that the Luftwaffe alone, if alerted, could wreak havoc among the hundreds of soft-skinned transport aircraft, each laden with paratroopers. As it turned out, only 21 American C-47s were lost in the initial invasion wave (8 more in the British zone), a fact that became Eisenhower's first sign of success that the airborne plan was working.

Even then, the paratroopers would be threatened with annihilation if the beach landings did not succeed, or fell too far behind schedule. It can be considered a stroke of fortune that most of the paratrooper commanders had lost radio contact and were out of touch during the initial hours of the invasion. A report from Maxwell Taylor, for example,

A famous blessing in front of the war memorial, which is draped with parachutes. (NARA)

A military band (right) greets American paratroopers as they arrive back in England, July 1944. The survivors of Normandy, if not in hospital, would enjoy several weeks of R&R, while their officers hastily trained thousands of volunteers to replace the fallen. (NARA)

that he could only find 30 of his men prior to first light on D-Day might have otherwise caused alarm. A notable feature of the battle was how badly scattered the paratroopers were after their nocturnal drop, though each unit gradually gained strength as wayward paras found where they belonged.

On D-Day, the 101st Airborne proved itself a magnificent fighting force in its first combat, the troopers either waging war on their own hook or relentlessly attacking their objectives under command. It was a battle where true qualities of leadership came to the fore, as sergeants found themselves commanding companies, and lieutenants temporarily led battalions. After the chaotic D-Day drop, and the even more nerve-racking glider missions, the 101st Airborne remained doggedly in the fight as frontline infantry, validating their hard training as well as their courage.

It remains as an irony that the overall mission of the 101st Airborne in Normandy, as well as that of its sister division, the 82nd, was to guard and ensure the successful seaborne invasion of Utah Beach. When the final tallies were in, the Allies only suffered 139 casualties on Utah, while the 101st Airborne suffered over 4,700 killed, wounded, and missing in order to help make that result possible.

It was only the start of a combat record that became unsurpassed in World War II, as the airborne would continue to serve as the cutting edge of the Allied drive to liberate Europe.

Further Reading

Ambrose, Stephen E. *Band of Brothers: E Company, 506th Regiment, 101st Airborne from Normandy to Hitler's Eagle's Nest*. New York: Simon & Schuster, 1992.

Beevor, Antony. *D-Day: The Battle for Normandy*. New York: Viking, 2009.

Griesser, Volker. *The Lions of Carentan: Fallschirmjäger Regiment 6, 1943–1945*. Philadelphia: Casemate, 2011.

Hastings, Max. *Overlord: D-Day & the Battle for Normandy*. New York: Simon & Schuster, 1984.

Marshall, S.L.A. *Night Drop: The American Airborne Invasion of Normandy*. New York: Little, Brown & Co., 1962.

Poyser, Terry, and Bill Brown. *Fighting Fox Company: The Battling Flank of the Band of Brothers*. Philadelphia: Casemate, 2014.

Whitlock, Flint. *If Chaos Reigns: The Near-Disaster and Ultimate Triumph of the Allied Airborne Forces on D-Day, June 6, 1944*. Philadelphia: Casemate, 2011.

Womer, Jack, and Steven C. DeVito. *Fighting with the Filthy Thirteen: The World War II Story of Jack Womer, Ranger and Paratrooper*. Philadelphia: Casemate, 2012.

Index

Also in the Casemate Illustrated series

Allied Armor in Normandy

An exploration of the Normandy invasion from the perspective of the Allied armored vehicles which includes over 40 profiles of tanks.

The 2nd SS Panzer Division Das Reich

The Das Reich Division was one of the most infamous units of the Waffen-SS, taking part in many of the greatest battles of WWII.

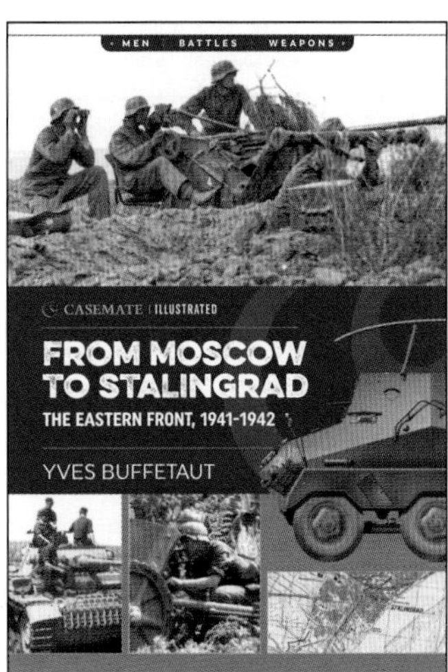

From Moscow to Stalingrad

The Eastern Front, 1941–1942

Numerous photographs of the vehicles and weaponry used by both sides, alongside detailed maps and text outlining the constantly changing strategies of the armies.

The Waffen-SS in Normandy

June 1944, The Caen Sector

This book examines the Waffen-SS in Normandy during the fierce fighting of June 1944, when they struggled to hold back the Allied advance on Caen.